"If it wasn't for Virginia Walden Ford, my kids would not have had the opportunities that they did. Her drive to fight for a better education for all children goes beyond what she accomplished in D.C. She is changing America's future."

Pamela Battle
Member, D.C. Parents for School Choice

"Virginia Walden Ford gave my family the tools to fight for school choice. She mentored and guided us every step of the way. She taught us that having the right to choose comes with a lot of responsibilities—and one is to help make sure that other children also have those opportunities."

Wendy S. Cunningham
Member, D.C. Parents for School Choice

"The D.C. Opportunity Scholarship Program is a shining example of funding what works for our children in education. It was inspired by parents who were demanding better educational options in Washington, D.C. Their inspiration was Virginia Walden Ford, who worked tirelessly to help these parents use their voices and absolute commitment to a better education for their children to get the United States Congress to act. I was proud to work with Virginia and John Boehner on this wonderful program, which continues to produce tremendous outcomes for those fortunate enough to participate."

Former U.S. Senator Joseph Lieberman

SCHOOL CHOICE:

A Legacy To Keep

A Memoir

VIRGINIA WALDEN FORD

BEAUFORT
BOOKS

For inquiries about volume orders, please contact:
Beaufort Books
27 West 20th Street, Suite 1102
New York, NY 10011
sales@beaufortbooks.com

Published in the United States by Beaufort Books
www.beaufortbooks.com

Distributed by Midpoint Trade Books,
a division of Independent Publishers Group
www.midpointtrade.com
www.ipgbook.com

Paperback ISBN: 9780825309397
Ebook ISBN: 9780825308215

Cover Design: Mark Karis
Interior Design: Neuwirth & Associates

Library of Congress Cataloging-in-Publication Data On File

Manufactured in the United States of America

10 9 8 7 6 5 4 3 2

Contents

Foreword

··

I HAVE ALWAYS LOVED TO learn. As a young woman, my mother and grandmother fostered my precocious spirit and constantly looked for opportunities to enhance my education.

By the age of 13, I couldn't get enough of science—specifically, chemistry. I would devour what I learned in class and long for more. As a result, my mother and grandmother started looking for more opportunities to stretch the boundaries of what I could learn and where I could go in life with that knowledge.

They found very quickly, however, that the sky was not actually the limit when it came to learning opportunities. Our income set the limit. Our income limited my opportunities to receive a quality education.

I first met Virginia Walden Ford in 2004. My grandmother and I were attending a local informational meeting about the D.C. Opportunity Scholarship Program. I had my sights set on Archbishop Carroll High School, which was known for its college preparation and high academic standards.

Miss Virginia, who was often referred to as "Mama" by the children who knew her, walked my grandmother and I through the scholarship application process and cheered me on as I waited to hear back on my application status. Thankfully, I received an Opportunity Scholarship, and not only did I graduate from Archbishop Carroll High School in 2008, but I earned a 4.3 GPA and was my class valedictorian.

From there, I attended Syracuse University and earned a Ph.D. in chemistry. I was the first person in my family to graduate from college. Today, I work as a postdoctoral oncology research fellow at Johns Hopkins University.

I owe my success to the D.C. Opportunity Scholarship Program—more specifically, to the support of Virginia Walden Ford. Miss Virginia gave my grandmother and I hope at that first meeting—hope that we could move beyond our current, narrow circumstances to a wide open future. Miss Virginia is not just a woman of words, though. She is a woman of action, directly responsible for the brighter futures of so many D.C. children and other children across the country who have been positively impacted by wider access to school choice options.

Educational opportunities for all children, particularly children from low-income and at-risk homes, is an American right. Miss Virginia understood that when she encouraged me and my family to advocate for what was best for me and my future. As you read the pages of this book, you'll begin to understand more about where Miss Virginia's drive and advocacy began—and why the movement she started two decades ago continues to gain momentum.

Dr. Tiffany Dunston

INTRODUCTION
"It Can Be Done and I Will Do It"

....

AS CHEMICAL REACTIONS, FIRES HAVE their own unique characteristics. Some fires burn brightly; others burn softly and slowly.

The flaming cross on my family's front yard burned with a vividness I can still see half a century later.

In February 1967, my father, William Harry Fowler, had just become the first black school administrator in Little Rock, Arkansas.

Today, the appointment of a black man to serve as the assistant superintendent of personnel for a public school district might warrant a brief mention in a local newspaper. But as the South's Jim Crow era neared its end, my father's job made national news. *Time* magazine wrote a profile, and syndicated columnist Drew Pearson wrote about my father's hiring in his Merry-Go-Round column, which at that time ran in 650 newspapers.

Local newspapers across the country also picked up the story. *Negro Educator Picks Little Rock Teachers* read the banner headline in the *Green Bay Press-Gazette* in Wisconsin.[1] *Negro Gets Little Rock School Post* read the *Quad-City Times* in Iowa.[2] In *The Philadelphia Inquirer*, the headline was *Little Rock Negro Takes School Post.*[3]

Little Rock had long been a hotbed of racial tension—especially when it came to schools. Still, a decade after the first students integrated Little Rock's schools after the Supreme Court's decision in *Brown v. Board of Education*, the idea of a black man serving as the school district's lead personnel officer—the person responsible for hiring all the district's teachers and staff—seemed earth-shattering to some.

At 44 years old, my father took pride in his hard-won position, but he did not consider his new job particularly controversial. Perhaps that's why the most accurate headline of that era came in the *Northwest Arkansas Times*: *Negro Sees Little Difficulty in Teacher Hiring Assignment*.[4] My father thought Little Rock had come a long way and stood poised for even more positive change.

"The progress Little Rock has made since 1957 certainly has set an example of what can be done in the area of desegregation," my father told the *Times*.[5] "It's one the entire nation could follow...I hope to place the best people where they will best serve, regardless of race. I have a very strong conviction that a school system is no better than the persons it employs."[6]

At the time, my four sisters and I had no idea that the hiring of my father for this position could offend someone. But many people in the South, including our town of Little Rock, still didn't like the idea of white and black kids going to school together. And they certainly wouldn't celebrate a black man's ability to hire both white and black teachers and school staff.

Our parents shielded us from the news stories and the gossip. However, our parents couldn't shield us from what happened on a cold winter night in late February 1967. Around 9 p.m., as we prepared to crawl safely into our comfortable beds for the night, a loud crash interrupted the tranquility. Our entire family rushed into my baby sister Renee's room to see what had happened. Broken glass lay on the floor from a large rock that had been thrown through the window and landed in Renee's crib.

Suddenly, we heard a commotion in front of the house. We rushed to the living room, pulled back the curtains, and looked out the front window. Blinded by flames and smoke, we saw a huge cross burning on our front lawn near the steps to our front door. The silent fury on my father's face was unlike anything I had seen before or since. He grabbed a rifle out of the closet, charged outside, and fired into the dark winter sky. But the men who had put the burning cross on our lawn had long vanished.

My mother clutched my sisters and I as we sat on the couch. Our home had an alleyway in the back that the Klan had accessed to get to the window where they threw the brick. Of course, they likely had no way of knowing that that room belonged to the youngest member of our family, but their actions had sent a clear message: We know where you sleep at night.

My father came back inside to see all of us crying—terrified about what had just happened. He hugged us, sat us down, and looked each of us in the eye. His face softened as he explained his anger to us. He talked to us about the civil rights movement and the changing world. But he also spoke honestly: "Girls, some people do not want to see blacks do well. But change will only come if you will stand up and fight for it."

Our parents were not hardened by the incident on that cold February night. On the contrary, they taught us not to take the bad deeds of the few out on the rest of the world. That evening, once we got back into our beds, I told myself that I wanted to follow in my father's footsteps when I grew up: to be courageous, dignified, and determined to carry on, persevere, and succeed—even when faced with the most challenging and personal of obstacles.

In February 1967, we faced real adversity. But even with a burning cross on our lawn, a rock in my sister's crib, and the national news focused on our family, my father remained undaunted. "The school board has pledged to desegregate each school staff as soon as possible," the Associated Press reported. My father was equally committed to desegregation, saying, "It can be done and I will do it."[7]

Little did I know then that my father's words would become my motto thirty years later, when—out of the blue—I would find myself in the center of a national storm regarding school choice and education reform.

And little did I know that a girl from Arkansas—the same girl who'd hid under her covers at night for fear of seeing another burning cross on her family's lawn—would one day sit across from the President of the United States in the Oval Office, arguing that black families should have the right to withdraw their children from the same types of public schools that my family helped integrate.

On that cold winter night, I had no way of knowing that years later, I would join with hundreds of other families—parents who looked like me and cared so deeply about their children's education that they, too, were willing to make sacrifices for it—to help pass an opportunity scholarship program for the nation's capital that would allow low-income children to escape failing public schools and receive tuition assistance to attend the private schools of their parents' choice.

Much has been written about the fight to bring school choice to our nation's capital city. But I witnessed it all firsthand through every setback, breakthrough, victory, failure, and redemption. And I know that the true story of school choice for Washington, D.C. schoolchildren centers around thousands of families—low-income moms, dads, and grandparents. It also centers around students that some had counted out but, when given a chance to learn, had risen to achieve great things. So many incredible elected officials and advocacy partners helped bring this story to life, but without the parents of Washington, D.C., this story never could have been told—because it never would have happened.

This book tells the story of those families. Although not strictly an autobiography—it doesn't include all the events of my life—it is also my story, based on my recollections. This book is the story of a girl who loved her mama, daddy, and sisters, grew up in the segregated South, became inspired by her parents' commitment to education and equality, and—when it came to her own children's education and that of so many other families—was determined to extend her family's legacy of advocacy and service. Quite simply, this is the story of someone who refused to take no for an answer.

"Negro Educator Picks Little Rock Teachers"
Northwest Arkansas Times
FEBRUARY 9, 1967

LITTLE ROCK, ARK. (AP)—"I do not anticipate a great deal of difficulty at all," says the Negro principal of an elementary school who has been given the job of hiring and assigning all teachers and other school personnel in the Little Rick School District. The principal, William Harry Fowler, 44, says "tremendous progress" has been made in the 10 years since Little Rock was one of the South's first battlegrounds on school desegregation.

"The progress Little Rock has made since 1957 certainly has set an example of what can be done in the area of desegregation," Fowler said Wednesday night. "It's one the entire nation could follow."

Progress Since 1957
The year 1957 was when former Gov. Orval E. Faubus ordered the Arkansas National Guard to block the court-ordered entrance of Negroes to Central High School here, and President Eisenhower sent federal troops to ensure the enrollment of nine Negro students at the school.

Fowler, who is expected to take over his new post by March 1, said the school district is under a court order to speed staff desegregation, and he intends to carry out the mandate.

"But I hope to place people where they will best serve, regardless of race," he added. "I have a very strong conviction that a school system is no better than the persons it employs. My main interest will be to continue to seek and employ the very best people available.

Board Pledged to Desegregate

The school board has pledged to desegregate each school staff as soon as possible, and Fowler said: "It can be done and I will do it."

Fowler was the unanimous choice of the Little Rock School Board for the District's $12,000-a-year post of assistant superintendent for personnel. It is the highest position ever held by a Negro in the city's school system.

The board appointed him on the recommendation of the school superintendent, Floyd W. Parsons.

Reprinted with permission of the Associated Press.

PART ONE | *Ringo Street*

1.

A Legacy to Keep

....

MY PARENTS HAD PREPARED FOR the challenging days of 1967 for their whole lives. You might even say that my ancestors passed a legacy of advocacy—the willingness to fight for what they believed was right—down to my parents, and my parents then passed it on to me. To understand this legacy, you need to meet my family.

Daddy grew up in Marion, North Carolina, the only son of Emmet Thomas Fowler and Esther Mae Fowler. In those days in the Jim Crow South, black people had no opportunity to get an education. My grandfather worked hard as a porter on a train, and my grandmother worked long hours as a domestic worker. Neither had gotten past third grade in their education, but they had bigger hopes for their only son. They wanted what all parents want for their children: better opportunities and a brighter future.

More specifically, they wanted my father to get a quality education. My grandparents knew that an education was the best chance my father would have to achieve more in his life than they did. But dreams often collide with reality. In Marion, black children could only receive an education up to the sixth grade. In 1935, during the height of the Great Depression, my grandparents scraped together what money they had to send my father off to Tuscaloosa, Alabama. They had heard that a school there, the Stillman Institute High School, educated black children beyond the sixth grade.

And so, my father traveled to Tuscaloosa and enrolled at Stillman. It wasn't easy for him, being alone at such a young age. He missed his family—and he struggled mightily. He paid his way through Stillman by working as a janitor, both before and after school, for seven long years. He wrote letters home when he could. And in their responses, my grandparents encouraged my father to make the most of the opportunity he had—the chance to get an education.

In 1941, my father graduated from Stillman Institute High School and Community College. That fall, he enrolled in Phi-lander Smith College in Little Rock, Arkansas, becoming the first in his family to earn a college degree. At Philander Smith, my father met my mother, Marion Virginia Johnson.

Uncle Nase

If the story of my father's upbringing stands as the quintessential story of perseverance and determination despite difficult obstacles, my mother's ancestors epitomize courage and the pioneering spirit.

My mother's great grandfather was a man named Nathan "Nase" Warren.[8] Born a slave in 1812 in Maryland, he moved to Arkansas in 1819 with Robert Crittenden, the man who "owned" him. Crit-tenden had been named the first secretary of the newly created Arkansas Territory that year, and news reports about his move from Maryland mentioned a six-year-old slave named Nase—my great-great grandfather. Crittenden was just twenty-two years old when he took Nase with him to Arkansas.

By the time of Crittenden's death in 1834, Nase had already worked out an agreement to earn his freedom. His new "owner," Daniel Greathouse, upheld the terms of that agreement. After his three-year enslavement at Greathouse's estate, Nase became a free man, even though his children and siblings remained slaves.

Twenty-five years before the Emancipation Proclamation, life for a former slave in the Deep South proved difficult. Public senti-ment against free blacks in Arkansas grew, especially because slave owners considered free blacks "troublesome" and "a nuisance."

But Nase remained determined to pursue success, and he even-tually took over a local confectionary. He and his delicacies quickly grew in popularity, with Little Rock elites calling on him to cater their weddings and other celebrations. He became known for his teacakes—a must-have at social events planned by the white women of Little Rock's high society. Nase used the money he earned at the confectionary to buy family members, including his siblings and children, out of slavery.

In 1852, Nase's confectionary caught fire—officials ruled it an accident, but Nase believed it was arson. Nase continued his business, but by 1858, the tide against free blacks in Arkansas had become dangerous, and Nase left the state for Ohio. He made the move at just the right time. In 1859, Arkansas lawmakers passed legislation requiring all "free Negroes" to exit the state or submit to a year of slavery. By 1863, Nase returned to Arkansas with his wife, Ida May. Together, they lived at 1012 Ringo Street, just a few doors down from the house in which I grew up.

The Reconstruction period following the Civil War saw many of Nase's family members and descendants rising to leadership roles. While living in Ohio, Nase joined the African Methodist Episcopal Church, or the AME. Nase brought his faith back with him to Little Rock and helped to build Bethel AME, where he became an ordained minister in 1882. The black folks in town called him "Father Warren," and the white folks called him "Uncle Nase."

Nase's influence extended even beyond the church, and his interest in politics grew after the conclusion of the Civil War. He participated as an official delegate to the Convention of Colored Citizens, held in Little Rock. At this first-ever political convention held by the black residents of Arkansas, the delegates showed up with a serious agenda—to ask the state "to grant us equality before the law, and the right of suffrage."

"We have earned it and, therefore, we deserve it; we have bought it with our blood, and, therefore, it is of priceless value to us," the convention stated.[9]

Six years before his death in 1888, Nase celebrated the birth of his granddaughter, Zola. And on October 7, 1922, Zola and her husband, Gordon Eliaza Johnson, welcomed their seventh child, my mother, Marion Virginia Johnson.

Gran, Mama, and Daddy

To my sisters and me, Zola was "Gran." She was a strong, sweet, loving woman and a true matriarch. She not only told us stories about her grandfather, but she served as the family historian—faithfully keeping a record of the family tree. In fact, much of what we now know about Uncle Nase comes from documentation saved and recorded by my grandmother in the family Bible.

Gran must have also inherited Uncle Nase's knack for baking. In fact, she always knew how to make our lives just that extra bit better with family recipes that kept bringing us back to the table. I have yet to find an apple turnover that comes remotely close to matching hers. Many of the women in our family have tried to duplicate the recipe; however, none have succeeded.

Gran was also a celebrated seamstress. By the time I got married, Gran was in her late eighties. My mother had made my wedding dress, but Gran thought it needed something more. So, I went over to Gran's house one day and found her stitching lace, by hand, on the hem and sleeves. Even though Mama had done a great job making the dress, the lace made it extraordinary.

After meeting in college, my parents dated and started planning for the future. However, like everyone from that generation, World War II interrupted their plans. Drafted in 1943, my father would serve in the army in World War II in Germany and Korea, but not before marrying my mother on August 8, 1944. My father served as a classifications specialist, was honorably discharged as a corporal in 1946, returned to Philander Smith, and graduated in 1948.

After that, my father took a job teaching in Pulaski County, Arkansas, eventually moving on to teach at an all-black public school in Little Rock. While teaching, my father continued his own education, earning a master's degree from the University of Arkansas in Fayetteville, Arkansas, in 1957.

My father became one of the first black students to receive a graduate degree from the University of Arkansas. Sadly, however, the school did not let him march with his class during their graduation due to his race. Instead, the university gave him a robe and his diploma and told him not to attend his own commencement.

Several years later, when my mother earned her master's degree also from the University of Arkansas, my father was determined that she would march at her own graduation. Did he ever smile when he watched my mother walk across the stage to pick up her diploma.

Despite their education, my parents continued to face racism throughout their entire marriage. That racism stemmed in part from a factor that some people might not fully understand today: As a lighter-skinned black woman, my mother faced discrimination for marrying a man with darker skin. My mother constantly had to prove that she was "black enough"—an incredibly frustrating burden for her given her pride in the family's history.

As a young married couple, my parents were once stopped by police in Roanoke, Arkansas. Believing my mother was a white woman, the officer arrested both of my parents and took them to the local station. At the time, the law prevented a black man from traveling with a white woman. My father and mother protested their arrest, with my mother pointing out that she was married to the car's driver. Eventually, my mother's father had to drive to the police station with my mother's birth certificate to prove that she was black. Only then did the police free my parents.

Aside from the many things they loved about each other, my parents shared a passion for teaching and education. My father would become the principal of several all-black schools in Arkansas and, as I described earlier, the assistant superintendent for personnel in Little Rock.

After earning her master's in elementary education, my mother went on to teach in the Little Rock school system. In 1965, she became one of four black teachers to integrate the city's white public schools. She taught for 28 years before retiring in 1984.

All these years later, my sisters and I still meet our mother's former students, who tell us what a difference her excellent teaching made in their lives. These conversations never surprise me because I know what a wonderful mother and teacher she was to my sisters and I. Along with my father, my mother taught us strong values and, above all, to do what is right and to make the most of every opportunity the Lord gives us, even when times are tough.

2.

Twins, Home, and Church

....

ON MAY 19, 1951, I came into this world—but I had some
company. My twin sister, Harrietta, and I arrived just six minutes
apart at an all-black hospital in Little Rock.

My mother had suspected she was pregnant with twins when
her small frame ballooned much larger than it had with our older
sister, Gail. She told her doctor that "multiples" ran in the family
history and that she knew there must be two children growing
inside her womb. In the days before ultrasound technology, however, each time a doctor or nurse checked for the baby's heartbeat,
they found only one. The doctors told my mother and father to
expect just one baby when the due date rolled around.

We now know, as modern prenatal technology can detect, that
Harrietta and I were mirror twins. We grew facing each other
in the womb, a common position for conjoined twins, which
resulted in medical professionals detecting only one heartbeat
for most of the pregnancy. About two weeks before our birth, we
had separated enough from each other for the doctors to detect
a second heartbeat. The doctors excitedly told my mother the
good news.

Unsurprised, my mother called my father at work to tell him
that her suspicions had proven well-founded. My father was so
shocked and overwhelmed by the news that he drove into a tree
on the ride home from work that evening. He was not injured,
but he definitely felt the pressure of preparing for an additional
child to come into his home in just a few weeks' time. The night
my mother went into labor, someone else had to drive her and

my father to the hospital because he did not want to risk having a second driving accident at such a crucial time.

The "Fowler Girls"

Harrietta and I were second and third in birth order. My older sister Gail had lived the good life for five whole years before her little twin sisters came along. Back in 1951, the rarity of twins gave us minor celebrity status. Photos of Harrietta and I graced our local newspaper, alongside another set born in the Little Rock area around the same time. Everyone wanted to see the miracle of more than one baby born at the same time and to the same parents. In 1954, my sister Doris came along, followed by the baby of the family, Renee, in 1962.

As one of five sisters, being one of the "Fowler girls" remains ingrained in my identity to this day. And when I wasn't referred to as a "Fowler girl," I was referred to as a "Fowler twin." I continue to embrace both of these monikers. I love being part of a large family of strong women and am grateful for my connection to my twin sister, Harrietta.

Harrietta was, then and now, my best friend. We always had each other's backs and were never lonely for other friends because we had each other. On the schoolyard, one of us would always come to the defense of the other if either of us found ourselves in an argument or fight. I almost pitied the people who had to contend with not just one, but two smart and strong Fowler sisters. That strong defense has never wavered throughout our lives. No matter what the issue is or who is on our case, we are there for each other, and our loyalty trumps everything else.

Since her teens, Harrietta's love for and commitment to children with special needs has been an integral part of her life. While most young people in high school focused on having whatever fun came to mind in the moment, Harrietta spent her summers working at a camp for children with special needs. The time she spent there ultimately led her to become an influential, amazing teacher for 30 years.

Harrietta never had children of her own, as she was busy with the ones already here who needed her love and attention. When I became a single parent of three, Harrietta was such a wonderful support for me—and my children have always thought of her as a second mother.

One Christmas, I could not afford to buy gifts for my kids. I explained to them before Christmas that our holidays would be lean, with no store-bought gifts. Their understanding made me even sadder, as I longed to give these beautiful children the Christmas that I felt they deserved. Many hours after they went to bed on Christmas Eve, Harrietta arrived from New Jersey—about three hours away from our house—with a car full of gifts for them. The next morning, she told my babies that Santa had brought the gifts.

Ringo Street

Growing up, my sisters, parents, and I all lived comfortably in our house on Ringo Street in a neighborhood of predominantly white families. Our brick home had five bedrooms: two downstairs and three upstairs. I loved spending time in the den upstairs, with its book-lined walls and telephone, studying and talking on the phone with my friends.

Thankfully, I grew up in a household that bustled with so much excitement, energy, and structure that all of our friends wanted to visit. My parents had no qualms about inviting people into our home, hosting women's club meetings, church prayer groups, card playing events, and more. When adults came over, their children would come, too, and we would all hang out in our den.

Our home also served as a haven for those children who needed parental role models like my mother and father. Neighborhood kids knew that our home was always open for visitors. My parents both believed that pouring love and kindness into the lives of children benefited not only the family unit but also the community as a whole.

Our big, happy family provided lots of opportunities for friendship. At the same time, growing up in a family with so many women forced me to create my own identity. It challenged me to recognize that I am not my sisters or parents, and they are not me. My life and choices belong only to me, and I extend the same courtesy to my family. We are individual human beings first.

A Changing World

As a young girl, I don't think I truly understood the gravity of how the world had begun to change around me. Looking back, I should have paid closer attention to some of the people who walked through the front door of our home on Ringo Street. In their own ways, these people ended up changing the world.

As respected community leaders and trailblazers, my parents served as networkers—willing and able to offer support, ideas, and assistance to other people who had committed their lives and careers to making Little Rock and our country a better place. Almost every week, somebody special visited our home to meet with and spend time with Mama and Daddy.

One of these visitors, local civil rights leader Daisy Bates, co-founded the *Arkansas State Press*—a publication that unapologetically published stories about racial crimes and pushed for progress through editorials. Bates is perhaps best known, however, for her work promoting and advocating for the integration of schools, helping shepherd nine students—known as the "Little Rock Nine"—to Little Rock Central High School in 1957. Bates' husband, journalist L.C. Bates, often spoke with my parents for his news stories, too.

Ralph Abernathy, one of Reverend Martin Luther King Jr.'s closest confidants, came to our home on a few occasions as well. As president of the Southern Christian Leadership Conference, he spoke with my father about how churches can advance equality.

Ozell Sutton, later the director of Arkansas Governor Winthrop Rockefeller's Council on Human Resources, also visited. Sutton wanted to understand how regular folks like my family were advancing integration and equality in the state. He came to my parents and their friends for advice on policies and to hear the truth about life in Arkansas communities.

Another visitor, Arkansas State Senator John Walker, opened one of the first racially integrated law firms in the South and zealously pursued civil rights cases. Back in the day, he would stop by our home on Ringo Street, a young, fiery lawyer with the desire to speak up and make change.

To my six-year-old self, the most famous visitor to my house looked handsome and important. Keep in mind, I did not understand many of the events occurring around me, especially as they related to school integration. One day, my parents told me that we would be having a guest stay at our house overnight. "He's an important man who is helping students get into school," my father told me.

When he arrived, I started talking with this energetic black man and asking him questions. "Virginia, you talk a lot," my father told me. Motioning to our houseguest, my father continued, "You could be a lawyer one day, just like him." Little did I know that our houseguest, Thurgood Marshall, would become a justice on the U.S. Supreme Court less than a decade later.

The fact that the "who's who" of people visited our home impresses me now, especially since I thought it unremarkable at the time. My parents remained humble people, but they viewed public service as a calling—one that they both took seriously.

A Commitment to Education
The feeling of home extended beyond the walls of our house. As a teacher, my mother would make a point of visiting the homes of each

of her students every year. She felt that going to their homes gave her insight into the lives of the children who spent so much time in her classroom. Mama would often say that a teacher can learn so much about her students by seeing the places where they live.

Once, Mama noticed that a little girl in her classroom always seemed sad and unfocused. Mama made an appointment to go to her home and meet her family. Once there, she found below-poverty conditions and realized that the little girl's attitude came from the stress of her home life and—on an even simpler level—hunger. While Mama could not change the student's home life, she was able to teach her more effectively because of the insight she had gained. And though my mother never specifically said it, I suspect she helped to feed the student, too.

As a result of her engaged attitude towards her students, my mother knew almost everyone in the community. People loved and trusted her because her students mattered to her—much more than the report cards she wrote or the paychecks she received. She wanted her students to succeed, and she put in extra time to invest herself in their lives.

My father had a lasting impact on the people he interacted with, too. He focused his efforts on helping kids in our neighborhood and his classrooms who faced more struggles than most. He believed in the community's role in helping to raise confident, strong, and educated young people.

Many years after my father died, I conducted a radio interview in the Wrightsville, Arkansas area to discuss school choice and my involvement in the cause. Upon meeting the radio host for the first time, he said to me, "I am the man I am today because of your father." He told me that he did not have a strong male role model growing up and that my father had served as his educator and coach. My father had encouraged this young man to stay on the straight and narrow, pursuing his education and living a life inside the law.

The host still credited the conversations he had had with my father, as well as my father's example, as the driving reasons he went on to experience his own success in life. "I knew I should tell you because I know he was too humble to mention it," the host concluded.

At my father's funeral, another man spoke to my sisters and me. He said that he had spent a few years locked up in prison, and my father had visited him once a month to offer him encouragement. Not only were we never aware of my father's actions, but none of us had ever even met that man before that date. That story summed up my father—and my mother. Both felt a responsibility to help even children who were not "theirs" have a brighter future.

A Calling

Some of my earliest memories come from the time my family and I spent in church. We attended White Memorial United Methodist Church in Little Rock and were very active in our church community, my parents serving as leaders, and my sisters and I involved in all aspects of Christian life.

Church for our family went well beyond just dressing up on Sunday mornings; we spent many evenings every week there, participating in group programs to better our church family and greater community. My mother taught Sunday School, and my sisters and I attended a month of Vacation Bible School every summer. And we didn't relegate Sunday church to an hour or two, either, instead spending the entire day at our church in worship, sharing meals, and spending time with the parishioners. Many of my early friends from those church days are still friends of mine today.

As a teen, I participated in the United Methodist Church Southwest Conference activities, and I was elected as the first female and first black president of the UMC Youth Fellowship in 1967.

Every year, our church hosted a Youth Christian Mission event at Thanksgiving. During this time, more than one hundred kids from other churches would arrive for an entire weekend of fellowship. At one of those retreats, I felt a strong calling to become a preacher. At just seventeen years old, I looked at the other students around me and felt an overwhelming desire to help guide them with the love and strength I'd felt my whole life as a member of my church and family.

At the time, however, women could not become preachers in the Methodist Church. After expressing my disappointment to Reverend Lester, he encouraged me to "listen harder" to what God was calling me to do. By the time women could join the ministry, I had gone to college and down another career path. However, the desire to reach youth in their troubled moments and show them hope beyond their circumstances never left me. In the end, while I may not have become a preacher by title, I never stopped speaking my mind, and I always tried my hardest to help others.

3.
Segregation and Discrimination

....

WHILE MY CHILDHOOD WAS FILLED with mostly good experiences, there were also some bad ones. Growing up in the South in those days, my sisters and I endured indignities that no adult, let alone young child, should have to go through.

The Ku Klux Klan (KKK) remained a fact of life in Little Rock during my childhood. Historians believe the first chartered Klan group came to Arkansas during the 1920s, with more than 7,800 members at its height.[10] Throughout the first half of the twentieth century, the KKK influenced local and county government—and occasionally made their presence known in our own neighborhood.

On February 9, 1960, as we sat in the living room of our house watching television, the whole world seemed to shake. Everything rumbled, as if a giant earthquake had rattled our neighborhood.

"What is that, Daddy?" I asked my father. He looked at me warily, then went to open the front door. Seeing no damage to houses nearby, he thought maybe a gas tank had exploded far away, or a very loud clap of thunder had startled us.

The truth proved more upsetting. A bigoted man who opposed school integration had placed two sticks of dynamite at the home of sixteen-year-old Carlotta Walls, who lived right around the corner from us.[11] He targeted Carlotta for only one reason: she was one of the nine black students attending Little Rock Central High School at the time.

My parents did not tell me what had happened; however, in the days after the bombing, I heard worried whispers in our house as my mother and father talked with neighbors about the violence that had occurred just a block away. "Thank God nobody was injured," I heard my mother tell one guest. While I did not realize it then, I would soon discover that even though our home life was peaceful and filled with love, in truth our happy family lived right at the center of a simmering cauldron of racial tension. Students like Carlotta, along with Harrietta, me, and our sisters, had sworn enemies we had never even met— people who hated us because of the color of our skin.

Separate

During my childhood, very clear boundaries existed between blacks and whites. My parents never explained the reasons behind those boundaries, as these would likely seem silly to a child. Black children in the South just seemed to inherently know that there were certain things they could not do and certain places they could not visit.

Looking back, I realize now that Little Rock was one of the more progressive areas in the South when it came to equality and civil rights. And I fully recognize that my middle-class family, with educated parents who had good jobs, had it a lot better than many—if not most—black families in the 1960s South.

But discrimination is discrimination. Blacks couldn't use rest-rooms in most department stores, still couldn't go out to eat at certain places, and had to avoid "whites only" water fountains. We had to sit in the balcony at movie theaters and couldn't visit certain public parks.

I also have vivid memories of the Ku Klux Klan's presence in Little Rock. One year, when I was around twelve years old, our parents told us that the KKK had obtained a permit to march down the street near our home to the Arkansas Livestock Grounds. Mama and Daddy told us to stay inside that day, but they did let us go visit our friend, Barbara, who lived up the street.

We could see the fairgrounds from Barbara's house, and we sat in her backyard and watched scores of people in white robes and strange white hats file into a place we'd visited many times. As little black children, we certainly knew about the Klan; however, seeing so many of them in one spot, so deliberate about their hatred of people like us on the basis of our skin color, really made the realization hit home. It was frightening but weirdly exciting to watch them in their robes, especially knowing their history. And believe me, every little black child knew about the Klan's history.

As my sisters and I became teenagers and civil rights expanded, we did see some positive changes. With that said, a part of me still questions, even to this very day, my permission to be certain places—even for a split second. I think that mentality remains among many southern blacks of my generation. We grew up being told that we deserved equal rights and treatment, and much of this has since been realized in our lives. However, we still retain the caution that accompanies our mentality to live without abandon or apology.

Up with People

The enactment of civil rights laws alone did not address the root problem that necessitated their passage: virulent racism.

During our high school days, Harrietta and I became involved in Sing Out Arkansas, a state group of the Up with People educational organization founded in 1965. Up with People worked to advance their mission of inspiring young people of different races and cultures to make a difference in their communities.

The Up with People campaign consisted of a group of hundreds of young people who traveled the world putting on stage shows, singing, and dancing to songs with themes based on their goals of freedom and morality. A racially integrated group, Up With People had a strong Judeo-Christian ethical message. The group sang songs like "Freedom Isn't Free," "What Color is God's Skin," "Joan of Arc," "You Can't Live Crooked and Think Straight," and "Sing Out."

During the winter of 1966, we traveled to Memphis to perform with "Sing-Out '66," a convention of all of the "Sing Out" groups from all over the South. As we travelled the backroads of Arkansas picking up kids, we all knew the dangers for an integrated group like ours. Even though the South had begun to change by that time, the Klan remained powerful and, along with other prejudiced and violent individuals, still posed a threat.

Our director, a young white man from New York, had never experienced the kind of racism that most of us kids had. On our way to Memphis, we stopped for gas and got off the bus to use the bathroom and visit the store. As we began to step off, gunshots rang out towards us. Clearly, someone was not happy that black and white kids were traveling on a bus together, and they did not want us in their town.

Our chaperones screamed for us to get back on the bus, and the bus driver hit the gas. We drove several miles, us terrified kids lying on the floor of the bus. Finally, we stopped. Nobody was injured, but the side of the bus was riddled with bullet holes. It was a frightening reminder that hatred, and the horrors it wrought, could lurk around any corner.

"Ya Lost?"

Another experience on small back roads in Arkansas proved instructive to Harrietta and me—and reminded us that even when you think bigotry is dissipating, it hasn't disappeared.

At the time, we were young adults, and Harrietta was dating a young man who coached at a rural high school in Arkadelphia, Arkansas, about fifty miles from where we lived. He had invited us to attend one of his games.

Halfway to Arkadelphia, Harrietta and I realized that we were lost. Too busy talking, we must have made a wrong turn—or several—on our way to the stadium. As we meandered along dirt roads in a heavily wooded area, we searched for signs of life and were desperate to ask for directions.

Eventually, we came across a small building that we assumed was a church. Cars and trucks were parked around it, and Harrietta and I thought we had conveniently stumbled upon a church service. This was a perfect place to ask for help getting back to the main roads—or at least, we thought it was.

When we walked through the doors, it took us a split second to realize that no, we were not in a church. And no, people weren't there to worship. We had walked into a Ku Klux Klan meeting, filled with men in white robes and those same hats that we saw from Barbara's backyard years ago.

Before we could gulp, gasp, or run, one of the men broke the silence. "Ya lost?" he asked us. We calmly explained that we were searching for the school and stadium. What happened next shocks us to this day—they gave us directions and let us leave! And you better believe we left. The realization of what had happened hit us a little later, once the "fight or flight" adrenaline had worn off. We never, ever told our parents about that night.

4.
A Political Awakening

....

FROM MY YOUTH UNTIL THE time I left home to go to college, my parents considered themselves Republicans. It may seem strange now, given that the majority of black Americans affiliate themselves with the Democratic Party. But in Arkansas in the 1960s, many black voters identified as Republicans for a simple reason: Even though Republicans at that time had their own flaws, the party of Lincoln proved far preferable to the virulently racist and segregationist southern Democrats.

In Arkansas specifically, Governor Orval Faubus, a Democrat, brought national attention to the state when he refused to integrate Little Rock Central High School. As the Associated Press described Faubus in a 1957 article, the governor hailed from a small town "where a man might spend a lifetime without ever seeing a Negro."[12] And he acted like it.

Faubus won six terms as Arkansas governor—often telling voters that they should choose him because he had "not sold out" to black residents and those who sought integration and equality.[13] When it came to our hometown of Little Rock, he didn't mince words: "There will be no enforced integration in the public schools of Arkansas as long as I am your governor."[14]

In 1964, wealthy industrialist Winthrop "Win" Rockefeller, who had only recently moved to the state, spent a lot of his own money trying to oust Faubus. But the segregationist governor held on to his seat, winning 57 percent of the vote.[15] On January 11, 1966, Rockefeller announced that he would again challenge Faubus for the governorship.

I was fifteen years old at the time, and my parents told us that electing Rockefeller represented a "now or never" chance for our state. We could elect a candidate with an imperfect record on civil rights—Rockefeller opposed the Civil Rights Act of 1964—or we could re-elect the same man whose racism brought violence to our community.[16] To our family, Rockefeller was the obvious choice.

My parents worked behind the scenes for his election. Given their positions in public schools, they couldn't say or do much politicking publicly, but in private, they worked to encourage our neighbors, black and white, to go to the polls and support Win Rockefeller.

The "Conceited Ass" Versus the "Prissy Sissy"

Eventually, Faubus decided against running for a seventh term. In his place, and with his endorsement, the Democrats nominated a man named Jim Johnson. Frequently described as a "fiery segregationist"[17] and "an unreconstructed state's-righter," Johnson said that if voters did not pick him, they would be stuck with "a prissy sissy," his nickname for Rockefeller.[18]

Unsurprisingly, personal attacks and dirty tricks marred the entire campaign. Rockefeller accused Johnson of stealing his personal financial records and countered Johnson's moniker of "prissy sissy" by calling him a "conceited ass."[19]

As a family, we followed this election closely—the good and the bad. Our house regularly buzzed with conversations about who might prevail and what it would take to get Win Rockefeller to actually *win* the election—and hopefully usher in a newer and fairer era for our state. For our family and for so many other black residents, Rockefeller presented "the most serious challenge [to the] Arkansas Democratic tradition since Reconstruction."[20]

Rockefeller and Johnson appeared to be neck-and-neck in the election. To try to gain an advantage, Johnson doubled down on racism and segregation. "The election of Jim Johnson in Arkansas would make the election of George Wallace insignificant by com-parison," he said, referring to himself in the third person.[21] Johnson railed against the "persecution of the majority" and described civil rights marchers as "a mess of trash."[22]

As *The Washington Post* described Johnson's candidacy, "He speaks this year only for the angry ones—the poor whites, the Klansmen, the people who would impeach Earl Warren."[23] Of Rockefeller, the *Post* said, "Rockefeller has another great asset this year: the Negro vote. To the Arkansas Negro...Rockefeller is by no means a civil rights champion, but unlike Johnson, he has not been endorsed by the Ku Klux Klan."[24]

On November 8, 1966, Rockefeller narrowly beat Johnson, "reaping strong support in Little Rock."[25] As the election returns came in, an aide to Johnson repeatedly said, "All is lost."[26] To our family—and to so many people across our state—the day after the election represented a major gain. Full of optimism, we hugged and cheered with each other. "This is big," Daddy told me.

That election in 1966 forever shaped how I viewed politics, politicians, and political allegiances. At the national level, President Johnson—a Democrat—promoted civil rights and pushed tirelessly for greater opportunities. But in my own backyard, Republicans held the mantle, albeit tenuously, of integration and fairness. I learned that year that working towards fairness, justice, and opportunity means working with people regardless of their party, especially on issues that matter to the local community. And it means holding leaders to account for their positions on issues that matter—again, regardless of their political leanings.

Courage in the Face of Tragedy

Win Rockefeller affirmed our confidence in him almost imme-diately after his election. He appointed more African Americans to positions of power in the state than any governor before him. My sister Harrietta later worked for him. And with his own quiet determination, Rockefeller also quickened the pace of school integration.

Always shying away from fiery rhetoric, Rockefeller accomplished near-impossible things, precisely because his reserved demeanor served as a cover for his desire to bring about change. While Rockefeller had his shortcomings and opposed federal civil rights legislation, he represented a vast improvement over Orval Faubus.

On the evening of Thursday, April 4, 1968, Harrietta and I came home from a church meeting. As we walked the few blocks back home, it seemed like a perfect spring evening.

When we opened the door to our home, my mother's tears as she watched the television immediately told us something was wrong. We looked at the set and saw the news: Dr. Martin Luther King Jr. had been assassinated on a hotel balcony in Memphis, Tennessee.

Harrietta and I dissolved into tears. My mother cried. My father, usually stoic, shed tears too. We had never met Dr. King, but to live in the 1960s as a black family in Arkansas—or anywhere in America for that matter—it was impossible not to recognize Dr. King's impact on our lives. "Who will take care of us now?" I asked Mama and Daddy.

The next day, five thousand people gathered outside of the state capitol building in Little Rock to memorialize Dr. King. Out of the crowd of black mourners, a familiar face suddenly appeared on the steps of the capital: Governor Rockefeller.

Rockefeller spoke with unusual eloquence about Dr. King's legacy and how together, we could build an Arkansas that "stands at the threshold of leading the nation in showing what people of good will can do."[27] Win Rockefeller was the only southern governor to memorialize Dr. King, linking hands with black leaders on the steps of the capital.

To put Rockefeller's principles in context, one need only read some of the editorials about Dr. King that had appeared in southern newspapers just before his death. For many whites, Dr. King was far from popular. "Dr. King has become a very dangerous man," one Louisiana newspaper editorialized, warning people to "watch out" because "There comes the Rev. King with his box of matches."[28] Saying that King's efforts in Memphis would prove "the trigger to a bloody confrontation" between whites and "the militant black masses," a Mississippi newspaper editorialized—or warned—that his "violence would be met with violence."[29]

Amidst our mourning for Dr. King, we saw political courage in our governor—not a perfect man, but definitely a statesman.

5.

The Second Wave

···

As you might imagine, my parents always stressed the importance of doing well in school and making the most of your opportunity to get an education. And I wish I could say that getting a good education was easier in those days. But Little Rock continued to struggle to comply with the new policy of integration.

Back in 1954, the U.S. Supreme Court, in its landmark *Brown v. Board of Education* decision, called racially segregated schools unconstitutional. Overturning its 1896 opinion that allowed for "separate but equal" facilities in the Jim Crow South, the Supreme Court rightly called "separate educational facilities" for different races "inherently unequal." In the years that followed, the National Association for the Advancement of Colored People (NAACP) traveled across the South, enrolling black children in previously all-white schools.

In 1957, nine black children sought to enroll in Little Rock's Central High School. When they showed up for their first day of school, the Arkansas National Guard barred the door—on orders from the state's governor at the time, Orval Faubus. Crowds of protestors turned out to protest integration, screaming out insults and awful names to the innocent children. The next day, President Eisenhower sent federal troops to enforce the desegregation order, and the children were able to attend school.

But these "Little Rock Nine" had a tough time in class, as southern Democrats slow-walked desegregation. Faubus continued to protest integration in the years that followed, even closing the city's public schools for two years. Once they reopened, a few more black children attended the formerly segregated public schools; however, most opted to continue attending all-black schools.

By 1966, Harrietta and I prepared to go to high school. Little Rock schools still had not fully integrated, even as the federal government pushed the state of Arkansas to continue desegregation. The state announced soon thereafter that more black students would attend Little Rock Central High School that fall. Harrietta and I wanted to attend Horace Mann Senior High School, an all-black high school that our older sister had attended. But we, along with 133 other black kids, were assigned to Central as part of the "second wave" of students to integrate the school.

Little Rock Central

When our parents told us we would attend Little Rock Central High School, we told them that we didn't want to go there. We had many arguments—which always ended with Mama or Daddy telling us, "You are going to Central, and that's the end of this discussion."

But in truth, it didn't end the discussion; as educators, my parents did not operate that way. Instead, they explained to us how during their youth, attending a school like Central seemed like an unattainable dream. They never got that chance, but now that the system had changed, we needed to seize the opportunity to get a quality education. They also told us that if we did not stand up and attend the newly integrated schools, it would affect our younger siblings and their own education.

My mother reminded us that many people had fought for the opportunity to show that black children could excel and thrive in the same schools as white students. While we finally began to understand the importance of embracing the educational opportunities we deserved, we remained uneasy.

I feared attending a new and unfamiliar school, especially with all the history and prejudice that the Little Rock Nine had experienced. Even though we fared far better than the horrors that those nine brave students endured, we still faced our fair share of racism and prejudice.

Some teachers ignored us and never called on us, as if we didn't exist. For example, while I had always excelled at math, I was devastated when I received a failing grade in geometry during my first semester at Central. Knowing that I would never fail math, my parents visited the teacher to ask about my performance. When the teacher claimed that I had never participated in class and that participation represented a large part of our grades, I told my parents that I had raised my hand many times, but the teacher refused to call on me.

The principal investigated the situation and discovered that the teacher had failed all of the black students, believing that none of us should have been there. Thankfully, the principal allowed me to retake the class, and I passed.

Unfortunately, my geometry teacher wasn't alone in thinking that we shouldn't have been there. Many of the other adults also did not give us a chance. And some of the students weren't much better.

One student called me a "nigger" under her breath every day. Our parents taught us not to react in those circumstances, but the comments hurt. Many of my black friends experienced similar situations, but we held our heads up and tolerated all the harassment. Many of the white students wanted to welcome us, but peer pressure from both students and adults often made them afraid to befriend us. The small number of black students in each class made socializing difficult, but we understood that we would never become friends with our classmates. Instead, we concentrated on doing well in our classes.

After many of the toughest days, I begged my father to allow me to transfer to Horace Mann. Each time, he gently but firmly explained to me that I had a responsibility to continue there, to set an example for my younger sisters. Eventually, I took that challenge seriously, and I vowed to stay at Central and do my best. Of course, Harrietta and I supported each other in this frightening new school environment—always believing that together, we could accomplish anything. We also took comfort in the friendship of the 133 other black students at Central, many of whom we had studied with in segregated schools since first grade.

Graduation and A New World

On May 28, 1969, Harrietta and I graduated from Little Rock Central High School. Standing there and receiving our diplomas with over 700 other students filled us with an incredible amount of joy. The look of pride on our parents' faces helped us understand that despite the difficulties of our past, it had definitely been worth it.

After graduation, Harrietta and I knew our next step was to go to college. While many black Americans of our generation became the first to pursue higher education in their families, Harrietta and I had the advantage of following in our parents' footsteps. In truth, there was never a question as to whether we would go to college. My parents took pride in the independent women Harrietta and I had become. They set high expectations for our continued education.

It meant, however, that we had to leave the tight-knit community in which we had grown up—a place where we felt largely protected and respected. I loved my sisters, parents, and grandparents, and felt cocooned in our lives together. That strong sense of family and purpose, though, also gave me the confidence I needed to set out on my own.

While I eventually accepted my parents' request that I attend and do my part in integrating Little Rock Central High School, I wanted to attend a Historically Black College or University. I had always had so much pride in my parents and other family members who had attended and graduated from HBCUs, and I felt that the same type of institution would be a safer place for me to set out on my own for the first time.

My parents researched the Hampton Institute, now known as Hampton University, in Virginia. Founded in 1868 by black and white leaders of the American Missionary Association to facilitate education for free blacks, my aunt had attended the school in the 1940s, as had my cousin more recently. My parents felt like Hampton would also be a good fit for me. I read up on this mysterious place, all the way in the Commonwealth of Virginia, and felt nervous and excited when I received my acceptance letter.

Leaving for Hampton meant leaving my parents, my childhood home, and Harrietta for the first time. Harrietta had been accepted to the University of Arkansas at Fayetteville, where she would pursue her teaching degree. During our high school years, we had discussed staying together and attending the same college, but in the end, we wanted to find our own identities. The idea of going somewhere completely new where no one knew my name, my father and mother, or any of my sisters terrified me, even as I recognized the potential I had there.

Leaving my home and my twin sister required me to summon a level of independence I did not know I had. Harrietta and I had been inseparable. Thankfully, our lives continued to intersect in the years after we graduated from college, and we almost always lived within easy driving distance of each other.

But I had no way of knowing any of that as I boarded the first airplane flight of my life to relocate as a young woman. My feelings of melancholy were overshadowed by the sheer excitement of navigating an airport, finding my own single seat, and getting ready to take off into a new adventure.

I thought about the advice my parents had given me throughout the years regarding my education. They had told me to recognize the opportunity of education and to work hard so that opportunity did not go to waste. I thought of all the times my dad had reminded me that I had a responsibility to be an example for my sisters and all the black children who would come after me.

I also had a feeling that leaving Little Rock was temporary. I knew that one day I would likely return because, after all, my entire family and life was based right there. My family and all the memories of my childhood lived in that home on Ringo Street. A lifetime of friendships and spiritual growth resided inside White Memorial United Methodist Church. A rich history lived in the family Bible my grandmother kept and the family stories we shared regularly.

While I always knew I'd return to my roots in Little Rock, I needed to spread my wings and learn more about the world outside that city's limits. I felt the desire to do something important with the long life ahead of me and do it with a greater purpose than mere self-satisfaction. So, even though I felt anxious about leaving, I wanted to see what life I could make for myself, by myself, in the larger world.

Emotions overwhelmed me as Little Rock grew further and further behind. Was I doing the right thing? Would I live up to the expectations of my parents, my sisters, and my community? What would my life look like in a few months? A year? A decade?

I had no idea what the future would bring. But from the spirit of my ancestors to the direct words of advice from my parents, I felt a strong responsibility to continue my family's legacy of advocacy. The first step was to take the opportunity of education seriously. As Little Rock faded behind the plane's drift, I embraced the future ahead and my responsibility to it—however it presented itself.

PART TWO | *Hawaii Avenue*

6.
Michael, Miashia, and William

....

In 1977, I moved to Washington, D.C.—a move that happened almost accidentally.

After graduating from our respective colleges, Harrietta and I moved back to Little Rock in 1975 and started working. I accepted a position at the Panel for American Women, an organization that studied the impact of social stereotypes. I loved my job, and Harrietta enjoyed hers, but something about staying in Little Rock bothered us.

On our own at college, we had each forged our own identities. But back home in Little Rock, we felt infantilized—though not by our parents. Because we had grown up in a tight-knit circle of friends and neighbors with parents who were prominent and well-respected in our community, people still referred to us as the "Fowler girls."

We took pride in that term, knowing how hard our parents worked to earn other people's respect. But we wanted to develop independent identities. We wanted to earn respect on our own terms—and frankly, we wanted a change of scenery, too.

One night, over dinner at an IHOP near our family's house on Ringo Street, Harrietta and I hatched a plan.

"Let's apply to jobs all across the country," Harrietta suggested. "And whoever gets a job first—we both move to that city."

I readily agreed, and we soon set out to apply for jobs across the country—in New York, California, Chicago, and Washington, D.C.

True to the plan, when I was offered a job at Sister Cities International in Washington, D.C., as an assistant finance manager,

Harrietta and I packed our bags and moved to the nation's capital. Mama helped us find an apartment, a sub-leased condo owned by one of her sorority friends. We paid rent there for several years before I moved to a brick rowhouse on Hawaii Avenue.

Motherhood

I spent twenty-six years at that house on Hawaii Avenue, a brick rowhome with three bedrooms, a porch, and a small backyard. It wasn't in the best neighborhood in D.C., but it certainly wasn't the worst, either. For me and my growing family, it was home. I spent most of my time on Hawaii Avenue either raising my own children or working with other parents and their children.

My oldest son, Michael, was a joy as a child. A loving and caring individual who exuded kindness, he and I developed an early bond that continues to this day. When other parents told me about troubles they experienced with their children, I always gave thanks that I did not encounter any difficulties with my dear Michael.

Michael had both intelligence and ambition—along with occasional bossiness—and his love of math and science resonated with me. When Michael graduated from a public high school in D.C. in 1992, he chose my alma mater, Hampton University, as his first-pick college—even though twelve other schools had accepted him. In 1997, Michael graduated from Hampton with a degree in finance and accepted a position at the London office of Pricewaterhouse.

My only daughter, Miashia, came next. Almost from the start, Miashia had a talkative, energetic nature—the type of child who could and would befriend anyone. For a while, Miashia had so many friends that I became known simply as "Miashia's mom." Whereas Michael excelled in math and science, Miashia loved writing. She edited the high school newspaper at Roosevelt High School in D.C., and in the eleventh grade, was accepted into a writing program sponsored by Time Warner.

Miashia and I butted heads from time to time during her teens—as moms and their daughters usually do—but we retained a close and loving friendship. We still talk multiple times a day, and I consider her—along with Harrietta—my best friend. Miashia graduated from high school in 1995 and went to Prince George's Community College to pursue an associate's degree in nursing.

My youngest son, William, had medical issues from birth—tumors in his mouth that made it difficult for him to learn to speak. His fragile nature led me to spoil him more than I should have.

While William acted lovingly towards me, to others he sometimes behaved like a brat. My son never had a cruel bone in his body, but that didn't mean he didn't cause mischief—doing everything from acting as a "superhero" by dressing in a cape and jumping off of our porch, to eating all of the Milk Duds that Miashia needed to sell for a school fundraiser, to trying to "get air" on his bike in the alley behind our house, Evel Knievel-style.

Saving William

The challenges William and I faced—the journey of a single D.C. mom and the son she adored—led me to my improbable school choice advocacy journey.

It all started one day on the porch of that rowhouse on Hawaii Avenue in the spring of 1997. I sat with a neighbor of ours, Bob Lewis, and explained the challenges I faced. William had just gotten in trouble with the police, and he was struggling mightily in his freshman year at Roosevelt High School.

As I told Bob that day, William's academic struggles had started many years before he got to high school. In elementary school, William's teachers told me something that still makes me shudder to this day. They called my son "incapable" of learning because of his speech issues. Not believing such garbage for one second, I demanded that they work to fix the problems. I visited his school frequently, politely asking for better options to address the challenges William faced. Over time, I became more persistent. But in all candor, my persistence got me nowhere.

As hard as I worked, William seemed destined to be treated as second-rate and defective. The teachers at his schools had stigmatized my sweet, talented son. I know that my mother and father, public school educators themselves, would never have approved of the way William's teachers treated him.

But even though it pained me to watch William struggle in school, I had a big problem: I had no other options to give him. At the time, Washington, D.C. required students to attend the schools in their own neighborhoods. Finding another school would mean paying private school tuition or moving to another area. I couldn't afford either of those choices.

I worked to surround William with the love and support that any child—especially one who is struggling—needs, but his challenges in school brought him down a dangerous path. I watched him align himself with the negative influences of our community. Drugs were prevalent around our neighborhood, and the drug dealers targeted our young boys to work for them with the promise of expensive items like shoes and clothes that they knew their single, struggling parents couldn't afford.

I saw my son choosing to run with this group of troublemakers. When I asked him why, he told me that he felt safer as a part of that thug world. William began skipping school and getting into all kinds of trouble with teachers and school administrators. He truly believed that hanging out with these miscreants would make him safe. He seldom did homework because he felt like it didn't matter to anyone whether he passed or failed. After all, his school teachers and administrators didn't believe in him, why should he believe in himself?

When William was eleven years old, one of his friends got

beaten so severely that he wound up paralyzed. During the assault, the boy's attackers repeatedly yelled at him, "You think you're so damn smart? You ain't smart!"

William's troubles worsened after that. One spring day in 1997, he came home with another suspension from school after having already received about a dozen of them.

"What am I going to do?" I asked Bob Lewis after I recapped William's struggles.

Bob had an immediate solution.

"We need to enroll him at Archbishop Carroll High School," Bob said, referring to the highly-regarded, private Catholic school nearby. "That's where I went to school. It's a great school, and it will give him a fresh start."

"There's no way I can afford a private school," I told him

"Well, how about this?" he offered. "I will pay half."

I sat there, mentally calculating whether I could afford my half of the tuition. I didn't spend too much time on the math, though, because I knew that William desperately needed a change of scenery—and, as Bob said, a fresh start.

"If you will really do this," I said to Bob, "I will do everything I can to pay my half. And thank you so, so much."

Night Cleaning Duty

That night, I sat at home and looked at the classified ads. I already worked full time at a nonprofit education and social services program called The Fishing School. My daytime hours were full—but I could find an evening job to help pay my half of William's tuition at Archbishop Carroll.

Eventually, I found a unique job at a local recording studio, which combined basic accounting work with after-hours cleaning. I worked from 9:00 p.m. to midnight. Between crunching numbers and scrubbing floors, I came home in the wee hours of the morning, bone tired. If I was lucky, I got a few hours of sleep before my day job at The Fishing School bright and early the next morning.

The hard work proved entirely worthwhile. From the minute that William enrolled in Archbishop Carroll, his behavior changed. In the first week, he began engaging with his teachers, caring about his schoolwork, and doing well. Quickly, he learned that he could perform more than jokes and pranks—he could also excel athletically and academically. When I asked him why his performance improved, he told me, "Mama, I feel like people at this school care about me. Before, the only person who cared whether I learned or not was you. Now, it seems like a lot of people care. Most of all, I feel safe."

William's almost-immediate turnaround brought me happiness and relief. But it was not altogether surprising. In the years since my older children graduated from D.C.'s public schools, the entire school system had deteriorated.

As *The Washington Times* wrote at the time, "more of the District's students are dropping out, their test scores have hit the bottom, bullets flying through the halls are replacing arcane spit balls and the school year keeps getting shorter."[30]

Another columnist noted, "The dismal record of D.C. schools is a national embarrassment. The city spends an average of almost $9,000 per year on its 125,000 enrolled students. This is the third-highest spending rate of any state or equivalent jurisdiction, some $3,000 above the average. Its student-teacher ratio (14.4 to 1) is the fourth-lowest of any state or equivalent jurisdiction. Yet SAT scores in the District rank 49th out of 51 (50 states plus the District), and its graduation rate is also 49th out of 51."[31]

As someone who grew up watching her parents fight to make sure that all children are given a quality *public* education, the entire situation depressed and enraged me. How could a public school system receive so much money and still fail to provide safe, effective education for children? How could the failure of these schools not demand immediate, no-holds-barred changes and reforms from city leaders? Why did elected officials seemingly do nothing while students languished in their learning and sat as prey for drug dealers and gang leaders?

Thankfully, William escaped. But I knew that many other students—far too many—were not so lucky.

7.

Getting Beyond Luck

....

BOB LEWIS' SELFLESS ACT OF offering William a partial scholarship that changed his life's trajectory had thrilled me beyond belief. My family, friends, and neighbors repeatedly told me how lucky we were. And indeed, we were lucky.

But something about the word *luck* shook me to my core. Should a struggling child's future rest solely on the improbability of having a benefactor like Bob Lewis step into his life and offer him a partial scholarship? Should mothers have to scrub floors at night just to make sure that their children didn't become victims of violence in school—or victims of educational malpractice in a well-funded but disastrously managed school system?

I didn't think so. But in reality, so many families couldn't get a partial scholarship like William did. Or, their parents were already working several jobs and couldn't get another one to afford private school tuition.

As someone who lived and breathed the fights over school integration in the 1960s, it became painfully clear to me that nobody would march, fight, picket, or protest to get their children *into* a school in Washington, D.C. In Little Rock, black families gave up a lot to get us into Little Rock Central, as Central had a great reputation. But parents in D.C., most of them black, wanted nothing more than for their children to *escape* the city's awful public schools.

In fact, I honestly doubt many black families would have had much of an appetite to fight so valiantly for school integration in the 1950s and 1960s if they had known that their children would be forced to attend schools that resembled the public school system in Washington, D.C., several decades later. Integration always served to promote justice and equality of opportunity, two things that the District of Columbia's schools didn't offer.

Surely, I wondered, someone must be working to fix these problems. But every time I read about education in the newspaper or watched a program about it on television, I heard the same broken record. Some politicians repeatedly claimed to have five- or ten-year plans to improve the city's schools. They frequently blamed their failure to implement those plans on a lack of funding. In reality, District schools had more than enough money. When those arguments fell flat, they simply blamed the federal government.

You see, in 1996, the federal government took control of D.C. government and its schools from local officials, placing them into receivership.[32] This drastic action took place because the entire government—not just the schools—had devolved into an abject disaster. From crumbling streets to missing money, the District of Columbia could not govern itself. And yet, some of the same District officials who had let these problems metastasize kept begging for more time, and more money, to make things better. "Once the federal government gives us back control over the city," their arguments went, "everything will get better."

Not only did I not believe their arguments but I did not have five years to wait. Neither did my friends and neighbors. After all, if the government fails to fix your streets, your car might get a flat tire. But a bad public education could ruin a child's life.

If you can't tell, I was outraged. Thinking back, the entire situation still enrages me. In 1997, I knew I needed to do something to help other kids like William—other students who didn't have the good fortune to escape a failing school and attend a better one. But I had no idea how to start. I attended D.C. Board of Education meetings and spoke up. I received a combination of blank stares and outright hostility.

A Phone Call

One day in the fall of 1997, my boss at The Fishing School handed me the telephone. "An organization called The Center for Education Reform wants to have a meeting with some of our parents," he told me. "Can you help them out?"

Founded by a woman named Jeanne Allen, the first-of-its-kind Center for Education Reform (CER) opened its doors with the specific goal of improving schools and creating better opportunities for children. The organization, and Jeanne, would fearlessly take on big bureaucracies; like me, they wanted immediate changes for children and families.

Picking up the phone, I spoke with a CER staffer named Mary. She explained that their organization was working with several Members of Congress to pass education reform legislation. Their bill would create an opportunity scholarship program so that low-income families in the District of Columbia could send their children to private schools. This simple proposal had the potential to change lives: Congress would set aside additional funding for the District of Columbia, and a nonprofit organization would use those funds to help pay tuition for low-income children whose parents could not afford private schools.

"Can you repeat that?" I asked. She told me that yes, the organization was working to promote the creation of a scholarship program that could literally have answered my prayers just a few months earlier—a program that could benefit so many children like William. To so many families, I immediately thought, this could be a lifeline.

Under the United States Constitution, Mary explained, Congress holds final authority over legislation in the nation's capital, including education programs. As a result, the scholarship legislation needed to not only pass the House of Representatives and the Senate, but be signed into law by President Bill Clinton. The city of Milwaukee had a similar opportunity scholarship program, and

Cleveland had just created one as well. If enacted by Congress, the nation's capital could follow in the footsteps of these cities with its own opportunity scholarship.

Mary asked me if I could organize a meeting of our Fishing School parents to inform them about the potential program. The Center for Education Reform wanted to find parents who could vocally support the proposal as congressional efforts to pass an opportunity scholarship program took shape.

I agreed to host the meeting, sending notes home with each of our sixty-five students. To my disappointment—and, I'm sure, to the CER's—my first attempt at bringing parents together to talk about school choice flopped. Nobody showed up to that meeting except for Mary and me. So we sat in a big, empty room and talked. She told me more about the scholarship proposal and the uphill battle it faced. I started opening up about my own experiences with William, and I told her about his scholarship.

As I talked, she looked more and more interested in my story. "You should tell your story," she said. "Members of Congress need to hear stories exactly like yours."

Mary and the rest of the team at The Center for Education Reform understood that the incredible power in personal stories and experiences. They knew that an advocacy organization could promote a scholarship proposal, but it would take the authentic, unfiltered voices of parents—parents who truly wanted the program—to convince elected leaders not only to support it, but to become passionately committed to the cause.

There was only one problem: I didn't like public speaking. While I had spoken publicly in the past, it wasn't my favorite thing to do. I became uncomfortable when the proverbial spotlight shined on me, preferring to interact with people one-on-one. But Mary made a compelling case, and I agreed to not only start talking about my experiences with other parents, but to help recruit other parents to advocate for the cause.

Congressional Action

From the minute I heard about the possibility of creating the opportunity scholarship program, I committed to working as hard as I could to help the legislation pass. But first, I needed to learn as much about the proposal as possible—as well as the politics behind it.

The proposal to create an opportunity scholarship program was relatively straightforward. The federal government would allocate additional money to the District of Columbia over and above what the District currently received. The funds would go to a nonprofit scholarship organization that would accept scholarship applications from low-income families, verify their eligibility for the program, and approve applications. Once approved, parents could select a qualifying private school for their children, and the scholarship organization would pay up to a specific amount of the tuition. In other states and news media, these programs are occasionally referred to as "school voucher programs." Regardless of the terminology, the proposal made a lot of sense, and it had the potential to change countless lives for the better.

Politically, the momentum for bringing a scholarship program to the District of Columbia had grown by the fall of 1997—and the effort had strong backers in Congress. House Speaker Newt Gingrich and Majority Leader Dick Armey were fighting tooth and nail to pass the initiative. Far from simply attaching their names to legislation as symbolic gestures, Gingrich and Armey wanted to use every possible legislative maneuver to get it passed.

"Thousands of children today in the nation's capital, at $10,000 a child, are being cheated," Gingrich told *The New York Times*. "They are being cheated by the politicians; they are being cheated by the unions."[33]Armey encouraged his colleagues to "soften your heart and get beyond the politics to help these very, very precious children."[34]

An unlikely set of allies in the U.S. Senate joined Gingrich and

Armey, including Senator Mary Landrieu, a Democrat from Louisiana. "Any under-performing district in the country would be a good place to experiment with vouchers for low- and moderate-income parents who, because of arcane rules and modest means, have no choice when it comes to educating their children," Landrieu told *The New Orleans Times-Picayune*. "So, D.C. would be one place to start, but clearly not the only place."[35]

Senator Joe Lieberman, a Democrat from Connecticut, became a key supporter as well. I was grateful to see that the proposal had bipartisan support.

But if opportunity scholarship supporters showed passion and enthusiasm, our detractors became downright vicious. Illinois Democratic Representative Jesse Jackson Jr. described the proposal as a modern-day "Tuskegee experiment."[36] When I heard his comments, I couldn't believe my ears. The idea that providing low-income children with access to the education of their parents' choice even remotely resembled the tragedy at Tuskegee—where "researchers" duped African American men into thinking that they were treating their illnesses with new medications, when in reality the researchers gave them no treatment at all and instead watched them die—sounded nothing short of revolting.

President Clinton also opposed the proposal. Claiming that the Administration "strongly opposes…private school vouchers," the White House issued a statement saying that the president would veto any spending bill that included the D.C. scholarship program. "Establishing a private school voucher system in the nation's capital would set a dangerous precedent for using federal taxpayer funds for schools that are not accountable to the public," the White House said.[37]

Republican Representative J.C. Watts, an African American from Oklahoma, issued the perfect rejoinder to Clinton's threats: "If the President can live in public housing and send his kid to private school, why shouldn't someone else living in the inner city, who lives in public housing, get to choose to send their kid to private school?" he told the *Los Angeles Times*.[38]

The supporters outnumbered the detractors, and on October 9, 1997, the House of Representatives passed a spending bill for the District of Columbia that included funding for the D.C. scholarship program. The bill passed by only one vote, "with the deciding vote cast by Speaker Newt Gingrich."[39] Despite my elation, we knew that the program's funding would likely be stripped out before the spending bill reached President Clinton's desk.

8.

Fighting and Organizing

....

IN LATE OCTOBER OF 1997, my son William and I sat down for an interview with Ron Hutcheson of the Knight Ridder Tribune News Service, which provides articles to newspapers across the country. Even though my father's history had made me used to seeing my family's name in the newspaper, seeing my name and photograph on the pages of faraway, well-circulated newspapers like the *Houston Chronicle* still seemed surreal.

"Driven by the fear that she will lose her son to the streets, Virginia Walden [Ford], a…single mother, is a fervent advocate of a pilot program in Washington that would provide financial aid in the form of school vouchers to help poor children attend private schools," Ron wrote.[40] And with that, my fight for school choice in the District of Columbia went national.

Over the next several months, the publicity continued—and so did our work. We visited offices, sent letters and postcards, and continued raising money. Our efforts energized me, increasing my desire to make a positive difference. But that still didn't stop the rise of a challenge that irritates me to this day: the argument that supporters of opportunity scholarship programs have ulterior motives, and that parents who supported these plans are just pawns for conservative politicians.

One union official, Lily Eskelsen of the National Education Association, ascribed mysterious motives to our congressional backers. "They have made this cynical, false promise to well-meaning, desperate parents," she said. "That is so dishonest, it is so low, I just want to slap those people."[41]

When I think back to that criticism, I always recall what one of our Democratic supporters, Representative Floyd Flake, told *The Los Angeles Times*. "Rather than look at vouchers as a right-wing, white conspiracy, look at them as an opportunity, because vouchers are here to stay," he said. "When a white person kills a black person, we all go out in the street to protest. But our children are being educationally killed every day in public schools and nobody says a thing."[42]

The Senate

In November, the Senate indeed removed the scholarship proposal from of the D.C. spending bill, as we had feared.[43] This removal stemmed, in large part, from the opposition of Senator Edward M. Kennedy, a Democrat from Massachusetts.

"I oppose the voucher amendments to the District of Columbia appropriations bill…The District of Columbia is not a test tube for misguided Republican ideological experiments on education," Kennedy said on the Senate floor. "Above all, the District of Columbia is not a slave plantation."[44]

Kennedy's words disgusted me. Allowing children to attend different schools—schools of their parents' choice—stood in direct opposition to slavery, in which masters brutally forced slaves to do things, and stay in places, against their will.

Senator Sam Brownback, a Republican from Kansas, countered Kennedy's heated rhetoric, pointing out that forcing children to attend failing schools—against their will—was fundamentally wrong.

"Should we require students whose families do not have the income to be able to move to other schools or to go to private schools to stay in this public school system?" he asked. "I submit we should not. It is not fair to the kids."[45]

Rebutting arguments that the scholarship proposal would "bleed money" from D.C. public schools, Senator Lieberman said:

"Good God, the system is bleeding. It is not this amendment that is bleeding it. What is bleeding is the failure of the system, and the blood that is being lost are the hopes and dreams of thousands of parents and children trapped in the school system who know it is a failure for them, who know it is not working for them."[46]

Despite these persuasive arguments in favor of the program, congressional supporters could not risk a veto of the entire D.C. appropriations bill. Instead, the Senate introduced, then quickly passed, the *District of Columbia Student Opportunity Scholarship Act of 1997* sponsored by Senators Joe Lieberman, Mary Landrieu, Sam Brownback, and Judd Gregg.[47] It was a "clean" bill—meaning that it was not lumped in with other spending bills.

Early Advocacy Efforts

As a native of 1960s Little Rock, I knew that nothing drew the attention of elected officials like a groundswell of support for an issue. I knew that if we could appeal to politicians' values and desire to remain in office, we would have a lever we could use to move mountains. We knew we would need to move those mountains in Congress and at the White House to get the House of Representatives to pass the *District of Columbia Student Opportunity Scholarship Act of 1997* and persuade President Clinton to sign it into law.

I didn't know how to get started until I heard a speech by Dr. Howard Fuller, an inspiring school choice pioneer and the superintendent of Milwaukee Public Schools. Dr. Fuller explained how parents in Milwaukee had fought alongside legislators and advocates to pass a scholarship program in Wisconsin. Successful advocacy, he said, required committed, visible parents willing to use the power of their collective voices. We needed an army—an army of parents.

Reluctantly, I had begun using my voice, but how would I get other parents to join me? To answer those questions, I turned once again to Jeanne Allen and The Center for Education Reform, which organized a half-day training session for parents who wanted to advocate for their children's education. Later, I received helpful advice from another urban reform pioneer named Robert Woodson. All the guidance I received pointed me in the same direction: I needed to get out into the community, leave my comfort zone, and start convincing one parent at a time to join our effort.

I first needed to become identifiable in the community so that I could bring parents together. I began to spend any spare time I could talking to parents and meeting with the pastors of small African American churches, searching for parents who would engage in this fight. I spoke at many meetings at small community organizations, tenant association meetings, and boys and girls clubs.

Frankly, anywhere I could get on the agenda, I spoke out, telling my story and encouraging—actually, begging—hundreds of parents to tell their stories and trust me. But as a new parent advocate, I had a lot to learn. Early on, my efforts to talk with parents about education reform fell flat because I struggled to connect my passion for scholarships with most parents' daily struggles.

I began my organizing efforts at a tenants' association meeting in a public housing complex. Looking back, I naively assumed that after my speech—which focused on the policy details of the proposed scholarship program—I would receive overwhelming support in my quest to build a grassroots army of parents who would stand with me to fight for quality education. After all, I knew I had faced my own challenges, trying to successfully raise my own children as a single parent, worrying about how to feed them on little money, and fretting over their safety in a community rife with drugs and crime. I knew the hopelessness and helplessness that other parents felt for their children's futures, having gone through similar situations myself.

To prepare for that meeting, I put on my best dress and prepared notecards of my key points. I walked into the room confident and poised. But as I looked out into the crowd, I realized that the trust I had expected would not come easily. For years, people had made promises to our community that had gone unfulfilled. How many other people in suits or dresses, reading from notecards, had made promises they hadn't kept? Too many to count.

Understandably, the same parents who so often heard about five-year plans, ten-year plans, and the insatiable need for more school funding hesitated to trust anyone. As I looked into their faces, I knew that I needed to stop *telling them* about the scholarship proposal and instead start *sharing with them*, explaining how school choice had changed my son's life.

I ditched the notecards. "Let me tell you about my son, William," I said. Only after I opened up, shared my story, and demonstrated our common bonds and goals did other families trust and join me. I realized I not only needed to build an army of parent supporters, I also needed to create an extended family—one where our lives could connect in more ways than just legislative fights.

I also recognized that to build this family army, I needed to work with people who had already won the trust of their individual neighborhoods. The pastors at a small church in our community recommended that I identify, seek out, and talk to women who the African American community refers to as "community mothers." These mothers and grandmothers babysat everyone's children for next to no money, mentored other mothers, and served as navigators for families experiencing hard times. I spent many nights sitting at the feet of these women, listening to their stories, learning their neighborhoods' histories, and humbly asking for their support. Once I earned that support and trust, our army and family grew exponentially.

Climbing the Hill

Our outreach to parents continued for several months. I never stopped working to bring parents into our organization. We did everything possible to help these moms and dads realize that we cared about their lives and their children's futures—while also explaining that we wouldn't be able to accomplish our advocacy goals overnight. The best thing that they could do, I told them then, was to recruit even more families to our cause. We knew that by building grassroots energy and resources, we could use our modest budget for professional advocacy efforts. We obtained our power by building a big, boisterous, diverse, and committed group of supporters. Once we built our family army, we continued adding grandparents and other supporters to our ranks, too. Not long after, my neighbors started referring to me simply as "the education lady."

Together, we kept growing our parent army. Eventually, we started visiting the offices of Members of Congress. At the beginning of the legislative fight, Capitol Hill staffers generally looked at our group as nice men and women who posed no threat. We went around in small groups from office to office, carrying ourselves with dignity and telling our stories to anyone who would listen.

In the early days of our advocacy, our parent army did a lot with hardly any money. The first donation to my organization came through a $50 check from my mother, followed by a $25 check from Harrietta. I didn't own a computer, so I often asked my friends to let me use theirs. Other friends volunteered to make photocopies.

One evening, our group met at one parent's home. We had thousands of postcards and letters that needed to go out in the mail the next day, before a critical hearing scheduled for the next week on Capitol Hill. Half a dozen or so parents set our kids up in the basement of the home with books and board games, and we set about getting our work done. At first, the work in front of us seemed overwhelming. However, as the night wore on, we started talking about our childhoods and singing some of the old songs from the civil rights movement. Time just seemed to fly by. At one point, I looked up and saw that all the children had joined us in folding letters and stuffing envelopes. We didn't have much money—but we had plenty of hope.

The entire school choice coalition grew in its efforts: aggressive advocacy on the part of parents; lobbying by our organizational supporters, led by The Center for Education Reform and the Institute for Justice; and tenacity by our allies in Congress. As for our opponents, their rhetoric grew more incendiary—and more ridiculous.

In *The Buffalo News*, columnist Carl Rowan described our proposal as "a wicked little sham," one that was "motivated not by love for the poor children, but by hatred of the public schools."[48] He concluded his vitriolic column by painting a portrait of low-income parents in Washington, D.C., as easily deceived vagrants or beggars: "I feel truly sorry for the poor parents…that they will grasp at this sham and delusion called vouchers."[49]

As expected, some black leaders also opposed opportunity scholarships—to put it mildly. One black pastor in Atlanta referred to supporters of our scholarship proposal as "demonic forces out to destroy public education."[50] Little did this pastor know that our parent group, some religious and some not religious, often prayed together—for our children's safety, for our community, and in hopes that God would watch over our supporters and bring wisdom and enlightenment to our opponents

9.

Votes and Vetoes

....

ON MARCH 12, 1998, I had the chance to tell my story in another way. I had previously attended meetings on Capitol Hill and spoke to newspapers and radio stations. But I had never testified before a congressional committee. The invitation to share my story before the House Committee on Education and the Workforce both thrilled and terrified me.

As that day approached, I could hardly sleep. I had written and rewritten my testimony a hundred times. As I sat in an ornate room at a long table in front of some of the most powerful men and women in the United States, I thought to myself, "How did this girl from Arkansas get here?" As I read my testimony, I was surprised to see that these powerful leaders looked interested in my message.

"After years of working in schools that my children attended and trying to be a parent who made a difference, I felt hopeless and helpless," I told the committee. "I remember that feeling so clearly…and I have heard it voiced many times from other mothers who have had nowhere to turn…I can't and won't say it enough—I will continue to say it—giving parents alternatives for their children's education is critical. We know our kids, and we know what'll work best for them."[51]

Another mother, Bernice Gates, also spoke, sharing a similar experience to mine. Bernice testified about how her son received a scholarship to attend a private school, which changed his life. "This is not public school bashing. I am a product of public schools. I am applauding every teacher that has ever taught me…but let's face it, folks are more concerned with the dos and don'ts of the school board than we are with our children learning."

By the end of our testimony, my fears had melted away. I felt empowered and proud. That moment had crystallized it all for me: No matter how poor you are, if you can get a platform and use it appropriately, you can make a difference in this world.

One person soon replaced that empowerment with anger: Eleanor Holmes Norton. First elected in 1990 to serve as the District of Columbia's non-voting delegate to the House of Representatives, Norton went to Yale Law School and had served in the civil rights movement. But she also received strong backing from local and national teachers unions, which opposed our proposal with a vengeance.

At the congressional hearing that day, she started by complimenting us and our commitment to improving education in our city. Her voice dripped with condescension, though. "Can I just say to...these parents how proud I am...of you. I mean, each of you have touched me in a very special way, and I know I speak for everyone in this room."

Then she turned cruel, interrogating me about whether I had attended public schools in the District of Columbia—as if my personal educational history would have changed my son's circumstances.

"I'm from Arkansas," I replied.

"I'm a fourth-generation Washingtonian who went through D.C. public schools," she shot back. "Ms. Walden, are you aware that under the bill that is before this committee today, you wouldn't qualify for any of that money because your children are already in private school?"[52]

On this point, Norton was correct. Under the terms of the scholarship proposal, parents of students who are already enrolled in private schools would not be eligible for scholarships. The purpose of that provision was to provide opportunities for children whose parents otherwise could not afford private schools. Unfortunately—even though I certainly could not have afforded private school for William without Bob Lewis' help—the provision meant that even if the scholarship program became law, William would not benefit.

To me, the provision was inconvenient. However, it did not weaken my resolve—nor did it disqualify my testimony. I knew that this fight went beyond my son. I did not want another mother to have to face the same challenges that I did. I did not want another family to have to rely on luck alone—on a partial scholarship provided by a neighbor after a conversation on a front porch. Most importantly, I did not want another child to be deprived of opportunities in education and in life simply because he or she comes from a low-income household. I had seen firsthand how having the opportunity to send my son to a better school changed his life, and I wanted other children to have those same opportunities.

Eleanor Holmes Norton could not seem to grasp that low-income mothers would speak up for a proposal that they themselves could not access immediately. "Put it on the record that neither of you are qualified!" she snapped.[53]

She then continued her questioning, asking whether a mother of a son in a private school was truly qualified to talk about the state of public schools in the District of Columbia. It seemed she was implying that perhaps we just didn't know enough or weren't trying hard enough.

As I explained, "I've been involved for years. I have three kids. I was an active parent. I tutored. I mentored….We care about all of the children in this city. I'm not going to sit here and be made to feel like my concern is *just* for my child. I worked real hard to stay in DCPS. I fought up at the schools, and talked to teachers, and worked with the principal, and I got tired of going up there and seeing knives pulled on my son and seeing him sit in a corner and not participate in things because he was scared."

"The bottom line is...are children getting the best we can give them? I don't want to wake up twenty years from now and some child of mine, or some child I [know], is saying to me 'Why didn't you all do anything about it?' That is why I fight."[54]

Nothing would stop Eleanor Holmes Norton from opposing us. No arguments, rationale, reasoning, or emotion would sway her. She was aggressive, and she was determined to embarrass me.

After the committee chairman gaveled the hearing to a close, I sat in my chair motionless—stunned, silent, and embarrassed. I could feel the tears starting to well up inside me. I ran out of that congressional office building as fast as I could—so that other parents wouldn't see me cry. At that moment, I regretted ever agreeing to share my story and testify. I wanted to quit.

But as I walked to the subway, my embarrassment turned to anger. "Hell, no, I won't quit," I thought to myself. How dare this woman essentially call my opinion worthless? How dare she tell any parent, let alone one of her constituents, that they were not qualified to talk about their own children's education? Did my parents quit their fight for integration after the KKK burned a cross on their lawn? No, they didn't. And if that didn't stop my parents, an angry woman sitting behind a dais wasn't going to stop me. Eleanor Holmes Norton wanted me to back down—to be complicit in a culture of silence that had destined too many kids to fail. Instead, I would dig in.

Faulty Logic

Both then and now, few people realize that local leaders should have easily accepted, even embraced, the D.C. scholarship proposal. Eleanor Holmes Norton's vitriol betrayed vulnerability and weakness.

In a traditional opportunity scholarship program, a portion of the money dedicated towards a child's public education will "follow" that child to a private school. Our allies in Congress offered an entirely different proposal. The federal government would provide *additional* funding to the District—separate from the funds the city had collected for public education—to pay for the scholarship program. That meant with the enactment of the scholarship proposal, the District would have *more money* for education.

What opponents like Norton feared, I believe, had nothing to do with funding and everything to do with optics. The sight of children and their parents lined up to apply for scholarships would serve as visual reminders to the entire world that families sought to escape the public education system in the District of Columbia. My willingness to sit before Norton and tell her—in public, no less—that parents wanted this program infuriated and embarrassed her.

Instead of letting those students pursue other environments where they could succeed—and instead of meaningfully fixing our local schools—Norton just wanted the entire discussion to end, as even *talking about* education in the District embarrassed her. So, Norton set an incredibly low bar for the performance of D.C. schools. Addressing the mother of a student who graduated from D.C. public schools, she said, "Tell me about the child who's graduated. Was that child so crippled in the D.C. public schools that he's now in the streets?"[55] If Norton defines a school system's "success" as preventing children from ending up "crippled" and "in the streets," that says a lot, doesn't it?

In the so-called capital of the free world, students dropped out of their schools in record numbers, too many kids could not read, and violence remained prevalent—despite the District of Columbia spending more money on education than anywhere else in America.

Years later, some local leaders, Norton included, said they opposed our scholarship proposal because they wanted to preserve "local control" and make sure that D.C.-related decisions were made by local leaders. But I knew that their arguments had nothing to do with "local control"—which, ironically, sounded a lot like the term, "states' rights" that southern Democrats used to defend segregated schools during the civil rights movement. The District of Columbia thrives on, and relies on, the federal government. Many of the District's residents work for the federal government, and D.C. leaders regularly ask Congress for all sorts of things—including money.

When local leaders talked about "local control," they really meant that they wanted discussions about the District's problems to remain under the radar. They focused not on the kids, or even the schools—but on the politics. Our parent advocacy efforts threatened the "if you don't talk about it, and you don't show it to people, it doesn't exist" mentality about D.C.'s educational failures.

Norton practically admitted as much in the hearing that day. "What about the rap on D.C. public schools? Up here people get on the House floor and they say that the D.C. public schools are virtually something for the sewer. The description of the D.C. public schools is such that it's language I don't think I'd want to carry back home."[56] She was right—because her constituents would have asked her why she hadn't fixed those schools.

Victory and Heartbreak

As we prayed and fought for victory, our organizational supporters redoubled their efforts, as did Speaker Newt Gingrich. He truly *got it*, asking opponents of the legislation to think of our plight. Would these opponents really tell children to stay in schools that their parents knew were not working for them? Would opponents tell children, "I know you may end up not learning how to read. I know you may end up a drug addict. I know you may end up the victim of violence. But no…stay where you are," he asked.[57]

On April 30, 1998, the House of Representatives took up the Senate-passed D.C. scholarship bill and approved it "after hours of passionate debate."[58] On May 8, it was sent to President Clinton for his signature.

Twelve days later, the day after my birthday, the president returned the bill—vetoed.[59] In vetoing the legislation, Clinton issued a scathing message, calling the creation of a scholarship a "fundamentally misguided" idea that would do "a disservice to those children." He claimed that signing the law would indicate a desire to "abandon" public schools. I felt devastated.

Clinton—who, again, would not enroll his own daughter in D.C. public schools, sending Chelsea to the prestigious Sidwell Friends School instead—did not understand that many families felt that our local schools had abandoned *us*. We did not want to destroy those schools; we simply wanted to force them to improve more quickly and give struggling students the chance to succeed in a different environment.

Later that day, I met with some of the organizations that had supported the legislation. "I will never do this again," I told them. "These parents believed me when I told them that we could win this fight. They worked hard, and we lost. How will they ever trust me again?" In my head, I wondered if I had turned into one of those public school administrators with their five-year plans, offering parents false hope.

Just then, a man named Clint Bolick, then the president and general counsel for the Institute for Justice, put his hand on my shoulder. "We lost one battle, Virginia," Clint told me. "Just one battle. You and your parent supporters have made it more likely that we can win the next battle. Your work has not been in vain. You have made a difference. And next time, Virginia, I think we will win."

But my anger remained. I channeled that outrage into an opinion piece that I wrote for *The Washington Post*. "I am all for saving the system, but I don't want to sacrifice my child in the process," I wrote. "Those who think that saving the system should take precedence over an individual child don't know what it is like to see a child begin to act like a hoodlum because of the school environment. They don't understand that a good alternative is out there for most low-income children—and at a price that is often less than the cost of educating that child in a D.C. public school."

My article ruffled some feathers and got attention—some negative, but most positive. Former Senator Larry Pressler called me at home to tell me that if I wanted to run for mayor of Washington, D.C., he would support my candidacy. Although flattered by the compliment, I declined. While I did not want to run for office, I also knew that I would not quit this fight.

Vouchers Deserved a Chance

By Virginia Walden Ford
Op-Ed for *The Washington Post*
MAY 24, 1998

I am a single mother with a son in 10th grade in the District. Last
year, when my son started having problems in and out of school, I
knew I did not want him to attend Roosevelt High School, a D.C.
public school that has a lot of problems of its own.

Thanks to a neighbor's help, I was able to send my son to Archbishop Carroll High School, where his grades have begun to
improve. My son still may be "at risk," but he is in a safe environment where he is learning, he is a star on his track team and he is
thinking about college.

The president recently vetoed a bill to give 2,000 low-income
D.C. parents the same chance my son is getting. The bill would
have provided as much as $3,200 a year to send these children to a
school of their choice. As someone who has seen what a difference
sending my child to a private school has made, I know that this bill
would have benefited many parents who face problems similar to
those that I have faced with my son.

Unfortunately, arguments against the bill focused on the need
to fix public schools. I am all for saving the system, but I don't
want to sacrifice my child in the process. Those who think that
saving the system should take precedence over an individual child
don't know what it is like to see a child begin to act like a hoodlum
because of the school environment. They don't understand that a
good alternative is out there for most low-income children—and
at a price that is often less than the cost of educating that child in
a D.C. public school.

Some people worried that poor mothers don't have the

knowledge it takes to decide what is best for their children. That offends me. I work as a mentor with many low-income parents, and I know that being low-income doesn't mean caring any less about a child's education. It doesn't take a doctorate in education to figure out that a child is going down the wrong path by hanging out with gang members and performing poorly in school. Parents shouldn't be blamed for a school system that doesn't know how to teach children.

Critics say my position on vouchers puts me in the same camp as right-wing conservatives. I am a lifelong Democrat, and I am not sure when the Democrats decided that siding with the poor and the needy is no longer part of their platform. School choice empowers parents, and I don't care who is behind it, Democrats or Republicans.

However, I do worry when Democrats think that spending more money on education is the only answer to problems in the schools. The District spends between $7,000 and $10,000 on each child in public school. To demand more funding and still produce terrible test scores is unacceptable.

Forty-one percent of D.C. public school third-graders and 53 percent of 10th-graders performed below a basic level on last year's Stanford 9 Achievement Test. Math results were even worse: 89 percent of 10th-graders scored below basic. With a record that abysmal, I don't see how anyone can think spending more money on public education is the answer.

Choice may not help every child, but if it means saving one child who would otherwise end up in jail or drop out of school, I think it should have been given a shot. The way I see it, those who opposed the vouchers—despite all the rhetoric—showed that they don't really care about low-income parents and even less about their children.

Reprinted with permission of *The Washington Post.*

Harrietta (L) and Virginia (R) in 1958, 1959, and 1970.

Photos: Author's personal collection.

Virginia, Harrietta, Grandma Esther, Doris, and Gail Fowler in Little Rock, Arkansas, 1957.

Marion Virginia Fowler and William Harry Fowler in 1967.

Photos: Author's personal collection.

Virginia in 1975.

The Fowler family
in 1979.
Top row, from left to right:
Doris, William Harry,
Marion Virginia,
and Renee. Bottom row,
from left to right: Virginia,
Gail, and Harrietta.

Photos: Author's personal collection.

Virginia's children.
Left side, from top to bottom: Michael Walden, Miashia Walden, and William Walden. Right side: William Walden in 2001 after enlisting in the U.S. Marine Corps.

Photos: Author's personal collection.

School choice supporters are interrupted by protestors at a rally on the day that Congress delivers opportunity scholarship legislation to President Clinton in 1998.

Virginia meets with House Majority Leader Dick Armey to discuss opportunity scholarship legislation in 2001.

School choice supporters and opponents hold competing rallies
outside of the U.S. Supreme Court Building in 2002.

Photo: Copyright © 2002, Associated Press, Rick Bowmer, Reprinted with License.

Throughout 2003 and 2004, families involved with D.C. Parents for
School Choice were a regular presence on Capitol Hill.

Photo: D.C. Parents for School Choice archives.

President George W. Bush joined Washington, D.C. Mayor
Anthony A. Williams (left) and U.S. Secretary of Education
Rod Paige (right) to advocate for private school scholarships for
D.C. schoolchildren at a 2003 event.

President George W. Bush greets Virginia at a 2004 event to celebrate
the enactment of the D.C. Parental Choice Incentive Act of 2003.

Virginia speaks about school choice at a Capitol Hill event commemorating the anniversary of the U.S. Supreme Court's *Brown v. Board of Education* decision.

Photo: Copyright © 2003, Getty, CQ-Roll Call Group Collection, Tom Williams, Reprinted with License.

African American leaders engage in civil disobedience at the U.S. Department of Education headquarters in 2009 to protest the elimination of the D.C. Opportunity Scholarship Program. From left to right: Darrell Allison, Dr. Howard Fuller, former D.C. Councilman Kevin P. Chavous, Virginia, Gerard Robinson.

Photos: D.C. Parents for School Choice archives

Senator Joseph Lieberman (D-Connecticut) talks with Nia Thomas, a student who was denied a scholarship after Congress acted to halt the D.C. Opportunity Scholarship Program in 2009.

Photo: Copyright © 2009, Associated Press, CQ Roll Call Collection, Reprinted with License.

Former D.C. Mayor Marion Barry, Virginia, and D.C. Opportunity Scholarship Program recipient Ronald Holassie march at Freedom Plaza in Washington, D.C. in May 2009.

Photo: D.C. Parents for School Choice archives.

The long, hot summer of 2009 was marked by rallies and demonstrations at the U.S. Capitol and the U.S. Department of Education headquarters.

Photos: D.C. Parents for School Choice archives.

An anti-scholarship protestor shouts at parents and students at the "Save School Choice" rally at the U.S. Capitol in the fall of 2009.

Photo: Copyright © 2009, Getty, The Washington Post Collection, Reprinted with License.

In 2011, House Speaker John Boehner successfully negotiated a compromise with President Barack Obama to protect and expand the D.C. Opportunity Scholarship Program. D.C. Parents for School Choice joined in celebrating the program's restoration and in recognizing Speaker Boehner for his efforts.

Photos: D.C. Parents for School Choice archives.

Virginia and her family. Top row, from left to right: William, Miashia, Jeremiah, Nikki, Michael. Bottom row, from left to right: Yamundow, Harrietta, Marion Virginia, Chloe, Virginia.

Photo: Author's personal collection.

PART THREE | *The Fight for Our Children's Futures*

10.
D.C. Parents for School Choice

THREE MONTHS AFTER PRESIDENT CLINTON dashed our hopes of creating a scholarship program for our children, I dug in once again. I recommitted myself to the fight for school choice by creating a new nonprofit organization, D.C. Parents for School Choice.

By advancing our work in a more organized way, I wanted to make sure that we would have the resources to go the distance in our fight and go toe-to-toe with our opponents.

At that time, I learned that John Walton, an heir to the Wal-Mart fortune and one of the leaders of the Walton Family Foundation, had personally donated to several school choice organizations focused on parent empowerment. Staff at the Heritage Foundation, a conservative think tank, encouraged me to request a donation.

In 1999, John Walton funded our organization with a $50,000 gift. As I soon discovered, once an organization receives one sizeable donation, support from other groups often follows. We wanted to use the money wisely while making as much of a positive difference for families—right away—as possible. That said, we thought it best to wait until after the 2000 presidential election, and the inauguration of a new president, to push forward again on a scholarship program.

In the meantime, we worked to educate parents about public charter schools. At the time, the District had just over a dozen public charter schools, public schools with more freedom to innovate in their curricula and practices. Our organization joined forces with another group, Friends of Choice in Urban Schools (FOCUS), to help raise awareness of these innovative new schools.

A Big Surprise

Even though I continued to work two jobs, advocate for school choice, and mother my three children, I often found myself strapped for cash in late 1998 and early 1999. Paying my half of William's tuition was becoming tougher and tougher. Between working and advocating for school choice, I was becoming physically and emotionally exhausted.

One day, before William's senior year, he and I sat down to talk at the kitchen table. Looking into his eyes, I knew he had changed so much—and for the better. He took his studies seriously, worked hard, and had stopped getting in trouble—and he remained the same loving, caring son I had always loved so much.

"Ma, I think I'm ready to go back to public school," he said to me. "It will just be for a year, and I will be fine."

I knew exactly what William thought. He wanted to give his mother a chance to take a break and give up one of her jobs. I also knew that he was ready to go back and even eager for the chance to prove himself. I would not send him back to Roosevelt, though. We found a school unavailable to him earlier, a public charter high school with a focus on building and construction. It perfectly fit a young man who could do anything with his hands and often volunteered to repair the bikes of kids in our community.

William thrived in that school during his senior year and graduated in the spring of 2000. On the day of his graduation, I drove to his school and sat in the car for a while by myself, reflecting on our journey together and William's success. I felt a sense of relief and an overwhelming feeling of pride and gratitude. Knowing that William had succeeded because of school choice gave me the motivation to continue my advocacy work—even though all of my children had now "left the nest."

As I took my seat at William's graduation, I didn't realize that the evening would have a surprise in store for me. When the school principal announced the graduates, he welcomed the valedictorian to give the ceremony's closing speech: My son, William Walden.

As William delivered a powerful, eloquent speech, I remained overcome with tears, cheers, thrills—and genuine shock and surprise. William knew that keeping his accomplishment a secret until the last moment would provide me a memory that would last a lifetime.

Back to the GOP

After growing up in a Republican household, I changed my registration to the Democratic Party. I'm not sure why I became a Democrat and left the party of my youth, but after working with congressional Republicans to promote school choice in the District of Columbia—and after watching President Clinton heartlessly veto our scholarship bill—it was not hard for me to return to the GOP.

As the 2000 presidential campaign heated up, I firmly remained in the Republican camp and rooted hard for George W. Bush. In many ways, he reminded me of one of the heroes of my youth: Win Rockefeller. Like Rockefeller, Bush wasn't the most eloquent campaigner—something both men readily admitted. Neither had a perfect record, at least in my eyes. But Bush, like Rockefeller before him, cared about people. I hadn't met the Texas governor, but I could tell that he'd support our cause.

It didn't hurt that Bush advocated for school choice and made education reform the centerpiece of his campaign platform, arguing that he would end "30 years of failure" in the country's public schools. [60] "Federal money will no longer follow failure," he said. "The federal government will no longer pay schools to cheat poor children."[61] In fact, Bush rolled out a plan that would provide $1,500 in federal scholarship funds to students across the country stuck in failing public schools—which was music to my ears.[62]

At the same time, I had a soft spot for one of the men on the Democratic ticket—the man that Vice President Al Gore chose as his running mate, Senator Joe Lieberman. In Washington, one could not find a more authentic, friendly, and caring man than Lieberman. One of the rare Democrats in the Senate who supported our scholarship program, Lieberman never wavered on that support—a fact that the media noted repeatedly at the time of his selection by Gore.

"Lieberman differs with Gore on numerous issues, such as his support for school-voucher programs," wrote the *San Antonio Express-News* in an editorial. "But Gore was right to reach out for a running mate with principles rather than seek someone with carbon-copy views on the issues."[63]

Lieberman acknowledged the differences. "Lieberman... said he supported vouchers but only for poor children and on an experimental basis," wrote Richard Locker in *The Commercial Appeal*. "He acknowledged that it was a point on which he and Gore disagreed."[64] But Gore continued to oppose opportunity scholarships for students stuck in failing schools. "I'm against them. I think they drain money away from public schools."[65]

Given that the views of the candidate at the top of the ticket usually trump the positions of vice presidential nominees, I stuck with George W. Bush. Despite my affinity for Senator Lieberman, I am glad I did.

Enlistment

My son William never ceased to surprise me. Around the time of the election, he sat down with me once again—with another bombshell.

"Mom, I know you aren't going to be happy with this," he said. "But today, I enlisted in the Marines."

I will admit that my response didn't lack candor. "The hell you didn't!" I screamed. "You're too young, and you're going to regret it."

We fought back and forth. Truthfully, I feared for my son, like any other mother would. But when he convinced me that he really wanted to enlist and serve his country, I gave him my blessing.

I went out and bought as many phone cards as I could afford, packing them with William as I took him to boot camp in Parris Island, South Carolina. Little could I imagine during those halcyon days of peace and prosperity in 2000 that a few years later, William would end up deployed overseas.

11.

A New President and a New Opportunity

....

AFTER GEORGE W. BUSH'S INAUGURATION as our nation's forty-third president, several key supporters of school choice moved into leadership positions in his administration. As secretary of education, Bush appointed Rod Paige, the former superintendent of schools in Houston. Paige, in turn, appointed my friend Nina Rees to run the Department of Education's Office of Innovation and Improvement, which oversaw federal efforts to support school choice.

One of the leaders considered for the education secretary position was a good friend of mine, Arizona Superintendent of Public Instruction Lisa Graham Keegan. Even though Bush ultimately selected Paige, Keegan also made the move to Washington, D.C., and created a new organization, the Education Leaders Council (ELC). That group advocated forcefully for our proposal and helped bring even greater national attention to the plight of D.C. schoolchildren.

The Oval Office

In February, President Bush announced that he would be proceeding with the opportunity scholarship plan he advocated as a candidate.[66] In April, the president's staff organized an Oval Office meeting with eight education leaders to discuss school choice. To my surprise and excitement, I received an invitation to attend the meeting on April 12, 2001.

Before we entered the Oval Office, two other invitees asked the rest of us to stay quiet. "Let us do the talking," they said. "We have some specific things we want to ask the president." I was content to take their advice, but President Bush wanted to hear from everyone. As we sat on the couches in the Oval Office, he went around the room and asked each of us about our work and our children. While I don't remember exactly what I told President Bush in the meeting—sitting in the Oval Office seemed surreal to me—I do know that a meeting that was originally scheduled to only last a few minutes went on for much longer because of the president's interest in the issue.

When the meeting eventually wrapped up, our group headed to the Eisenhower Executive Office Building. President Bush would deliver a speech about school choice to several hundred parents assembled there.

As we walked out of the Oval Office, I whispered to another mother, "This looks exactly like it does on *The West Wing*," referring to the popular NBC drama starring Martin Sheen as fictional president Jed Bartlett.

"I think so, too," I heard a voice say from behind me. It was President Bush, who had apparently been listening to our conversation. I couldn't believe it. Not only had I just attended a meeting in the most important office on the planet; now, President Bush had struck up a conversation with me. I almost had to pinch myself to remember that I wasn't in the middle of a bizarre dream.

As we continued walking, President Bush asked me more about my life. I told him that I had a twin sister, and he told me about his twin daughters, Barbara and Jenna. Even as the most powerful man in the world, with the weight of the world on his shoulders, he truly cared about me and my family. I would never forget that kindness.

Once inside the Eisenhower Executive Office Building, President Bush spoke forcefully to the attendees about the need for education reform and school choice.

As *The Washington Times* reported, the president "reiterated his belief that children who attend public schools that do not help them learn should have the option to move on to other public or private schools that help them excel."[67]

"America's schools are increasingly separate and unequal," he said. "And that is unacceptable in our great land. We must do more than tinker around the edges. We must all come together and fight for real reform and real change."[68]

September 11, 2001

Five months after that meeting, on September 11, 2001, terrorists attacked the United States. Like everyone in America, the attack left me shaken. I felt devastated for the families of the Americans who had died that day, and grateful for the heroes who had rushed into burning buildings and saved so many lives.

I also thought about my own family. My son Michael had, just months earlier, left his job at Goldman Sachs in Manhattan to work as an actuary at a church in Richmond, Virginia. Had the attack happened just months before, who knows what could have happened to him?

And I thought about William, still in boot camp on Parris Island but scheduled to graduate soon. After he left boot camp, where would he go? The nation seemed inexorably headed to war.

In the days after the attack, my thoughts migrated to the families in Washington, D.C. Many knew victims of the Pentagon tragedy, and the sight of tanks on the streets of our nation's capital disconcerted us all.

The work of our government shifted dramatically, too. Domestic policy issues took a backseat to foreign policy. Our families at D.C. Parents for School Choice prayed fervently for our country and for our president.

The Power of Parents

Even as we mourned and worried, our work as parent advocates continued. We knew that eventually, domestic policy would once again become a priority. And so, over the next two years, we worked to build an even stronger army of parents and grandparents willing to fight for their children's and grandchildren's futures—the true heroes in this story.

Over those two years, I met some of the most extraordinary people—remarkable individuals who had already given so much but would sacrifice even more if it meant a better opportunity for their children and grandchildren.

One grandmother, Catherine, who was raising her grandsons, would do anything necessary to ensure that the boys received the best education possible. Even though we spent incredibly long hours walking the halls of the Congressional Office buildings, she showed up day after day, anytime I called. Despite her fear of public speaking, she stepped up whenever we needed a speaker for an interview, a hearing, or a meeting—whatever we needed, she delivered. Catherine never complained about the heat, the rain, or the hours. She trusted me and wanted to help make sure that we achieved our shared goal.

Another parent leader, Valerie, was faced with terrible personal issues—the potential loss of her home, a search for employment, and a troubled teen son—but she insisted that her young daughter would have a chance to get a quality education. Often through tears, and despite all kinds of obstacles, she told me time and time again that she would do whatever we needed to accomplish our goals.

Barbara, a single mother of two, faced a layoff and an awful financial predicament when, in the middle of the campaign, she learned her six-year-old son was deaf. Despite this devastating news and the stress she experienced working within a difficult system to get him help, she kept fighting beside us for this program every time we called. Her children had received private scholarships, so she knew the importance of this program for other low-income families and remained determined to get it passed.

Together, we worked neighborhood by neighborhood to raise

awareness about the benefits of the opportunity scholarship proposal. We visited elected officials, held informational events, wrote letters and postcards, and shared our stories with news media. It was hard work, but it was rewarding. Working together to advance a shared cause built a bond between all of us—one that transcended advocacy for a specific policy. We were truly a family.

Opportunity Scholarships Reemerge as a Priority

Eventually, our hard work started to pay off. On April 16, 2002, Representative John Boehner held a hearing about private school choice programs and invited me to testify. Less than a year later—in February 2003—Representative Jeff Flake reignited our hopes for school choice in the nation's capital, introducing a new bill to create an opportunity scholarship program. When I talked to Representative Flake about his legislation, I asked him a simple question. "Do you really think we can succeed this time?"

"Yes," he told me. "Because this time, we have parents who will support the bill, a coalition of people who will work to pass the bill—and a president who will sign it."

This prediction proved correct. For our part, we worked hard to make the press conference announcing the new legislation a success. Representative Flake's office asked me to send "a few" parents to the event. We sent dozens.

"Parents who want a choice are driving this, and parents, not Congress or teachers unions or city officials or anybody else, ought to decide where and where not to send their children to school," Flake said at the news conference.[69]

Around the same time, President Bush announced that he planned to include $75 million in his 2004 budget for scholarship programs in five cities, including Washington, D.C. To build support for the proposal, Secretary of Education Rod Paige met with D.C. leaders, including Mayor Anthony A. Williams and D.C. Councilman Kevin P. Chavous, on February 5, 2003.[70]

A day after the meeting, Williams and Chavous spoke out in opposition to the scholarship proposal but indicated their willingness to continue their discussions with Secretary Paige.[71] To us, that meant that our school choice proposal remained alive—and that we could still win support from local elected officials. It was a step forward.

While the politicians strategized, our parents enthusiastically wanted to show public enthusiasm for school choice. We kicked our advocacy efforts into high gear by launching a petition drive to show support from families across the District for the scholarship bill. We wanted to persuade both Members of Congress and local leaders in D.C. who would influence them.

At a parent meeting, I passed out blank petition forms to the parent leaders in our group, asking each of them to commit to getting one hundred signatures by the next week. I knew that this group of parents would stop at nothing to get the job done. One mother even waited in line at the local jail, where children lined up to visit their incarcerated parents. She got each of these parents—mainly fathers—to sign the petition. Eventually, a guard at the jail approached her, prompting her to worry that she had violated a rule by asking prisoners to sign the petitions.

"I heard what you were talking about," the guard said. "And I want to sign that petition myself. I have children in these schools, and we deserve better." Eventually, our petition grew to 3,000 names.

Iraq and Afghanistan

In April of 2003, I received a call from my son, William. I knew this call would eventually come, but nonetheless, I had deeply feared it. Just weeks earlier, President Bush had launched Operation Iraqi Freedom. "Ma," William told me, "I'm being deployed to Iraq."

I sent William away with as many AT&T phone cards as he could pack, and he called me every chance he could. But in a faraway place, working hard and in dangerous conditions, William sometimes was unable to contact me for weeks. From the moment he deployed until the day he got home, I cried every single night. Every night on the news, when anchors talked about Marines dying in Iraq, my body stiffened.

In 2004, during the First Battle of Fallujah, I worried night and day that something had happened to William. Each morning, I waited to hear footsteps on my Hawaii Avenue porch, petrified that a military "notifier" would knock on my door and tell me that my son had been killed. Three weeks after the battle concluded, William called me, safe and sound.

William spent ten months in Iraq, followed by five more months in Afghanistan. When he finally returned to the United States in 2006, many of my friends joined me to greet him at the airport in San Diego. He remained stationed in San Diego until his honorable discharge. We wanted to celebrate his service—and that of the other brave young men and women whose courage and sacrifice represented the very best that our country has to offer.

My fellow mothers and I had lived through the Vietnam era, where our brave soldiers suffered horribly upon their return— blamed for decisions made by politicians. We were committed to giving our sons and daughters the heroes' welcome that they deserved.

As William's plane landed and the Marines disembarked, I craned my neck to get a sight of my son. But I couldn't see him.

Suddenly, I heard a voice. "What, Ma, don't you recognize your son?"

It was his voice. But the man standing in front of me was just that—a man. When William left for his overseas deployment, he weighed 160 pounds. The day he returned, he had packed on so much muscle that he was indeed practically unrecognizable. He came home tougher than he left, but just as kind as always. Most importantly, my child was safe.

Virginia Walden Ford Testimony
"Equal Education Choices for Parents" Hearing
U.S. House of Representatives
Committee on Education and the Workforce
April 16, 2002

Thanks to a neighbor's financial help, I was able to send my son to a private high school, where his grades and attitude immediately began to improve. He has now graduated and is serving in the U.S. Marine Corps.

I still shudder to think how very different his life would have been had he not been able to attend a school that offered a strong academic program and an environment that inspired him to succeed...For years, D.C. parents have been told to wait, and reform would come. But is it right to sacrifice the educational future of our children by waiting four more, or six more years and seeing no changes, or changes that come so slowly they are impossible to see?

I lead D.C. Parents for School Choice and counsel many low-income parents, and I know that being low-income does not mean caring any less about a child's education. We hear from parents who have bright children but those children are behind in reading and math.

Children in some of the worst high schools in the city have begun to acclimate themselves to the "dropout" culture that pervades their schools. They will begin to expect to drop out the way many of their friends have...In our neighborhoods, when young males drop out, they will often end up in prison or worse.

I have been working on this for a long time and have testified before. The more you are involved in helping parents, the more you realize how many parents are desperate for alternatives and need help. It is getting worse, not better.

12.

Tremors and Earthquakes

....

THE MONTHS BEFORE AND AFTER my son's tour of Iraq in 2003 were among the most stressful and emotional months of my life—and not just because of my son's deployment to a war zone. Back in Washington, D.C., our school choice proposal set in motion a series of political earthquakes that forever changed education in the District of Columbia.

The tremors started on March 15, 2003, when more than one hundred parents braved serious transportation delays in the District to pack a special meeting held by D.C. City Councilman Kevin Chavous on school choice in the District of Columbia.

With the support of Councilman David Catania—an early supporter of opportunity scholarships—dozens of parents made the case for passing Congressman Flake's bill. "If Uncle Sam wants to foot the bill for a school choice program, I suggest we take it," said one mother, a public school PTA president.[72]

At the end of the meeting, Chavous once again indicated his openness to working with the federal government on expanding school choice in the District.[73]

As for me, I rejoiced that parents' voices were being heard. Paradoxically, for years we had found eager audiences on Capitol Hill, but local leaders had largely ignored our proposals. Chavous' meeting moved us in the right direction—and yielded almost immediate results.

The Dominoes Fall
On the morning of March 29, 2003, I woke up to a stunning article

in *The Washington Post*, an opinion piece by Peggy Cooper Cafritz, the president of the D.C. Board of Education. A prominent leader in the African American community, Cafritz had initially opposed our proposed scholarship program. In her column, she not only reversed her opposition but went a step further, arguing that passing the program would benefit D.C.'s struggling public schools.

"We should join the U.S. Department of Education in forging a system that includes vouchers, charter schools, and public schools – one that would afford children in the District the best possible education," Cafritz wrote.[74]

Even when you spend every waking moment working on a project, some things still surprise you. I had no idea that Cafritz planned to support the proposal, and I later learned that she agreed to endorse school choice at the urging of local business leaders. Her endorsement only began the acceleration of the momentum behind school choice.

On May 1, 2003, D.C. Mayor Anthony A. Williams stunned city and federal officials alike by announcing that he, too, had reversed his position and would support a private school choice initiative for the city. Not only did he reverse his position, he wholeheartedly backed the effort—speaking in favor of the opportunity scholarship program at an event with Secretary Paige and Peggy Cooper Cafritz. "I fully and strongly support the initiative to bring scholarships to this city," the mayor said in his speech. "We will find that our regular public schools will end up in better shape."[75]

Days later, Chavous endorsed the proposal, too, saying that "No school bureaucracy will reform itself internally. It only comes through pressure. And the most effective form of pressure is choice."[76] And just days after that, Cafritz, Williams, and Chavous all testified at a hearing of the House Committee on Government Reform, speaking in favor of Flake's bill.[77]

Meanwhile, Representatives Tom Davis and John Boehner introduced their own school choice legislation. That brought the number of proposals to advance scholarships for D.C. families to three: the Flake proposal, the administration's budget plan, and the Davis-Boehner bill.

Eleanor's Lonely Battle

All this activity in favor of school choice left one person seething with anger: Eleanor Holmes Norton. As our parents joined Mayor Williams, Peggy Cooper Cafritz, Councilman Chavous, and congressional Republicans to champion the school choice proposal, Norton worked overtime to sow resentment and sabotage opportunity scholarships.

As conservative columnist Michelle Malkin wrote in her syndicated column, "Eleanor Holmes Norton is stark raving mad. The congressional delegate...accused her fellow Democrat, D.C. Mayor Anthony Williams, of 'selling out' last week because he supports a Bush administration-backed school choice proposal that would free thousands of poor black students from rotten public schools."[78]

When Norton held an anti-scholarship rally at a local school, I brought two dozen parents to the event so that she could tell us in person why she opposed greater opportunities for our children's education. She and her staffers literally slammed the door in our faces, refusing to admit us to a public event at a public school. As someone who had lived through the fight for school integration as a child, having yet another schoolhouse door slammed in my face—and this time, by a black woman—stung.

Writing in *The Washington Times*, columnist and editor Deborah Simmons wrote that Norton's frustration "does not grant Mrs. Norton the right to stand Orval Faubus-like at the schoolhouse door. That is precisely what she did last Thursday...Mrs. Norton was there under the pretense of a new pro-school choice but anti-voucher coalition. But, when two dozen honest pro-choice parents came knocking, Mrs. Norton denied them entry—ugly shades of Arkansas Gov. Faubus and the National Guard in 1957. 'There is no more important civil right than the right to a good education,' says one of the shut-out moms, Virginia Walden Ford.'"[79]

Hitting the Hill

Truthfully, Norton's opposition only energized us to fight harder. And the increased local support from Williams, Cafritz, and Chavous also galvanized many of our supporters to redouble their efforts.

An informal group of organization leaders regularly met to help advance the scholarship proposals. Calling ourselves the "D.C. Coalition," the group included a representative from the Archdiocese of Washington, representatives from independent private schools, nonprofit organizations like CER, the ELC, Children First America, the Institute for Justice, the Milton and Rose D. Friedman Foundation, and the American Education Reform Council. Local business leaders, most notably real-estate investor and philanthropist Joe Robert, used their considerable local political ties to help advance the effort, too.

The coalition met regularly to strategize and to update one another on events in our particular areas of focus. Some members of the coalition lobbied directly. Others focused on talking to private schools to make sure the schools had sufficient space for scholarship recipients. Still others worked with legislators and local politicians to help draft proposed legislation. I worked to organize the voices of the parents most affected by school choice in the District. Of course, the more people who came out, the more we could demonstrate community support and the greater our influence on the Hill.

Working with a coalition is exciting. It can also be challenging.

With so many groups now involved in the fight, I felt stuck in so many meetings to discuss the latest developments at the city and congressional levels and to develop strategies. At one point, I felt like I was spinning my wheels—talking to the same group of people again and again at meetings, but not reaching the real decision-makers on Capitol Hill.

Finally, Robert Enlow, an executive with the Milton and Rose D. Friedman Foundation and one of the members of the coalition, recognized my frustration and listened to me as I vented. Then he gave me the advice I needed to pull me out of my funk.

"You need to go out and do what you do best," he told me. "Don't let these meetings stop you from moving the ball forward. You and the other families are all so passionate about this issue, and it could actually impact your lives. Go to the Hill and tell your stories!"

Robert was right! As a result, D.C. Parents for School Choice decided that regardless of which legislation would ultimately reach a vote, we would make our presence known each and every day on Capitol Hill.

Thousands of families wanted the school choice proposal to pass. And so, for ten months, we visited Capitol Hill every day. Every morning at 10:00 a.m., I arrived on the Hill with about two dozen parents to walk the halls, show our faces, and talk to legislators.

Day after day, we repeated the same routine. We always wore white T-shirts emblazoned with "D.C. Parents for School Choice," so that nobody could mistake us for tourists. We stopped in as many offices as we could, scheduled meetings with Members of Congress, and went to any and every hearing related to education.

Most of the time, different parents joined the Hill meetings each day. Understandably, low-income parents had difficulty taking time off of work—leading to a loss of income—to meet with Members of Congress. Thankfully, we knew—regardless of which parents could attend each day—that we could always count on a young woman named Liz Moser. She joined us each and every day on Capitol Hill. As a staffer at the Institute for Justice, a nonprofit law firm, Liz did everything from holding babies while parents met with Members of Congress, to buying lunches, to helping us prepare for meetings. She became like family to both me and our parent advocates.

As we spent more time on the Hill, we began to get more attention in the press and support from various members of Congress. One time, I took about fifty parents to meetings in congressional offices. Our group purposefully split up, with small groups of parents visiting different offices, so that we could have the most impact possible. At one point during that day, I got a telephone call from an education staffer who worked for one of our supporters in the Senate. "Everyone on the Hill is talking about your group," she told me. "We cannot believe you managed to bring *hundreds* of parents to the Hill today alone!"

While we had thousands of supporters across the District, we only had a few dozen parents visiting offices that day. Still, we liked to hear that we were making an even bigger impact than we had hoped.

13.

Hardball

....

As we quickly learned, running a successful advocacy campaign takes money. The costs of copying, T-shirts, and postage alone were expensive! The parents and grandparents advocating for the scholarship proposal were sacrificing time off of work to support these efforts; some were even helping us pay for the tools we needed to advocate for the scholarship proposal. Even so, it quickly became clear that to sustain our efforts, we needed larger donations.

After John Walton's initial investment in D.C. Parents for School Choice, and after we built our parent army, we became prominent enough in the school choice movement that donors with resources started coming to us unsolicited. In fact, one individual contacted us to make a sizeable anonymous donation.

Two months later, after we had spent about half of the money, our anonymous donor's representative called and asked me to do and say some things about education that I didn't agree with. Instead of simply going along with their wishes, I sent back the remaining dollars—much to the donor's shock. Wouldn't our little cash-strapped organization do anything for money? No, it wouldn't.

But other donors trusted our work and let us parents call the shots. For example, I met a representative of Indianapolis businessman J. Patrick Rooney on the steps of the U.S. Supreme Court in 2002—at a rally that we helped organize to cheer on the parents and lawmakers who had created a school choice program for Cleveland, Ohio. With Cleveland's opportunity scholarship program under challenge before the court, school choice advocates from across the country gathered in solidarity. The event, one-part rally and one-part reunion, united parents—mostly black and brown moms—from cities across the country.

When Mr. Rooney's colleague approached me and asked me to tell him about my work, I didn't know what to think. I explained what I did, and a few weeks later, Mr. Rooney called me. He told me that he admired our efforts and he wanted to provide as much support—including financial support—as he could. From that day until the day he died in 2008, I had the honor of calling Mr. Rooney a friend. He and John Walton never told our parent advocates what to do, what to say, how to think, or who to work with. They trusted us.

Another early donor to our efforts was a woman from Michigan named Betsy DeVos. A shy lady who resolutely believes in the importance of school choice—and who has spent time mentoring children and providing personal scholarships to them while advocating for education reform—she now serves as the U.S. Secretary of Education.

Rallies

With local leaders' support secured, our coalition recognized the importance of continuing the momentum for the scholarship proposal by keeping our cause in the news. With the national press corps focused on so many important issues across the country and around the world, we had to think creatively about ways to keep our story, and our fight, in the news.

To maintain momentum and obtain publicity, we planned rallies on Capitol Hill. Instead of covering legislation written on a piece of paper, we knew that the news media would show the faces and tell the stories of people who wanted our legislation passed. Simply having parents tell the truth made for better articles and television stories.

Over time, we learned how to plan rallies in an organized way. Initially, however, we remained so focused on our mission that we were unaware of all the paperwork needed to hold a public rally on Capitol Hill. In other cases, we simply didn't have time to get permits.

At one of these impromptu rallies, we thought in advance that we might face arrest for protesting without a permit. But we moved forward with our plans regardless. As I walked out the door on my way to meet a busload of parents revved up and ready to attend a rally, one of our organizers took me aside and said, "Virginia, we raised the bail money, so you can stop worrying about it."

The cash brought some comfort, but it didn't totally calm my nerves. Who wants to tangle with the police? Nobody, and especially not single parents who have just managed to cram one more "to do" into their already incredibly busy lives. We boarded the bus, and, once on the road, I turned to our front line activists and said, "Look, this is serious. We could be arrested today because we don't have a permit. If you don't want to participate fully, I understand. But we do have bail money, and—" Before I could get the rest of it out, they all started talking at once. "I can go to jail," one woman said to her friend, "but you'll need to pick up my kids this afternoon, so don't get yourself arrested. Who else is in that part of town? Okay, they can all go over to my mother's for the night, if need be." Everyone immediately started figuring out how they could help one another and still finish the job they'd committed to do.

No one got arrested on that day—or any other day. We had spent so much time on Capitol Hill that the Capitol Police knew us. They'd seen us come day after day in our D.C. Parents for School Choice T-shirts, sometimes with our children. We frequently met in front of the Capitol to eat, regroup, or get assignments to go to other buildings.

The day of this particular rally, one officer smiled and told me how he had watched us over the months and how much he admired our persistence and passion. He'd have to report us, he said, but it might take him a while to get through to the office, so we might be gone by the time he got back, right? I smiled in gratitude for the warning and made sure we had left before he returned.

Spending Bills, Again

In the summer of 2003, lawmakers combined the Davis-Boehner scholarship proposal into a larger spending bill—also known as an appropriations bill—for the District of Columbia. This meant that if the bill passed, Congress would send D.C. money for the opportunity scholarship program—in addition to the rest of the money it was allocating to the city. Just like in 1997, congressional leaders believed that adding the program into the spending bill would increase its chances of passage. But our experience in 1997 also taught us that adding the program to a spending bill had its risks, as lawmakers had the power to remove the program from the bill at the last minute if they wanted.

The change also meant that the opportunity scholarship proposal would no longer be under the jurisdiction of the education committees in each chamber of Congress; rather, they would be under the appropriations committees. Instead of testifying before legislators who focused on education, our parents needed to talk with the legislators who discussed money and spending.

In the House of Representatives, Representative Rodney Frelinghuysen served as a key member of the House Appropriations Committee. Because of his role in assigning funding to the scholarship program, we stopped in at his office to reinforce its importance to parents. The Congressman was in the lobby of his office when we went to visit him, so he invited us into his personal office. His staff found chairs for all the parents and students, and he gave each of us a small bag of candy. We talked with him for an hour, and he listened to the stories of every parent and child who wanted to talk. The next day, we learned of his commitment to funding our scholarship program in the larger appropriations bill.

In addition to visiting undecided lawmakers and supporters— who we wanted to thank for their support—we also made it a point to show up at offices at which we knew the lawmakers opposed our efforts. We did not expect that we would change their minds, but *you never say never.* It also gave all of us personal satisfaction to see our opponents squirm while we acted in such a dignified, professional way.

These visits included one to Eleanor Holmes Norton's office. When we walked in, one of her staff members said that the Delegate would only meet with the adults who showed up, not their children. Norton didn't want the kids in the meeting, implying that they wouldn't behave themselves. But our kids knew better. They knew how serious our visits to the Hill were, and they acted with dignity at all times. Sometimes, they took that seriousness a bit too far. That day in Norton's office, these four- and five-year-olds picked up magazines to pretend to read; they didn't realize, however, that they were holding them upside down. Their mothers just laughed.

Appropriations hearings brought even more unique and interesting experiences for our group. Even though these meetings with Members of Congress seem dignified on the surface, the atmosphere often became circus-like, with some Members using hyperbolic language to describe the scholarship proposal. During one particularly long House appropriations markup, about fifty parents attended and listened as members of the Congressional Black Caucus assailed the scholarship proposal.

The name-calling that day infuriated me. Men and women who looked like me, who shared my commitment to racial equality, and whom I respected as political leaders, condescended to us and condemned our cause.

Whenever we took parents to the Hill, we always observed one rule: We didn't start until 10 a.m. so we could give parents time to take their children to school, and we made sure that they returned home by 2:30 p.m. so that they could pick their children up. As the lawmakers ridiculed our proposal and our intentions, we realized that the time had come for parents to pick up their children from school. So, because children truly do come first, we left the hearing. The next day, people asked us if we had walked out of the hearing to protest the Black Caucus lawmakers' comments. In a way, we did—because we never lost focus on the people who truly mattered: our own children.

On July 15, 2003, the House Appropriations Committee voted to approve $10 million for the D.C. Opportunity Scholarship Program as part of a $7.9 billion D.C. appropriations bill, a significant step forward in our movement.[80]

A Knife in the Heart

The Senate Appropriations hearings provided their own drama. When the District of Columbia spending bill reached the Senate Appropriations Committee in late July, our parent group took solace in the fact that we had allies from both parties. Senator Mary Landrieu had repeatedly assured us of her support. We had no reason to doubt her; along with Senator Joe Lieberman, she had co-sponsored the scholarship proposal that President Clinton had vetoed in 1998.

We met with Landrieu's staff late in the afternoon the day before a committee meeting. Her staff told us that she remained committed to supporting the creation of a scholarship program. But by 9:00 a.m. the next day, everything had changed.

At the meeting, Landrieu attempted to torpedo the scholarship proposal with a "poison pill" amendment that would have dissuaded many schools from accepting scholarship students and effectively neutered the program before it even started. When her amendment failed, she suddenly decided to oppose the proposal that she had originally helped conceive back in 1997.

Needless to say, Landrieu's reversal shocked our parents—including me. We waited in the hallway after the meeting, some of us crying. When Landrieu walked past us, a young boy named Mosiyah Hall asked her where she sent her children to school. "Georgetown Day," she replied, referring to one of the District's most elite—and expensive—private schools.

"But," Landrieu continued, "you will never be able to go to that school with this scholarship program." She implied that a scholarship of $7,500 would not cover the full amount of the tuition, but the way she delivered the message left our group feeling shattered.

That evening, I called my friend and supporter, J. Patrick Rooney. "Mary Landrieu just drove a knife in our hearts," I said to him. "I don't know how we can win this thing if we lose more votes, especially from supporters."

Rooney's response made a lot of sense. "Landrieu thinks she can say and do anything in D.C. and that nobody in Louisiana will ever know or care," he said. "We need to let them know what she said."

We decided to take out a full-page ad in *The New Orleans Times-Picayune*, the largest newspaper in Louisiana, the following week. Our goal was to inform Louisianans of Landrieu's out-of-touch, elitist reaction to Mosiyah's question. Mr. Rooney agreed to pay for it. Some members of the D.C. Coalition simply wanted us to ignore Landrieu's about-face on our scholarship proposal. But we took Landrieu's actions—and words—personally. Plus, we knew that holding one senator accountable would help prevent other senators from also double-crossing us. If elected officials wanted to lie to us, we had to play hardball.

As I later explained to *The New Orleans Times-Picayune*, "We always felt that Mary Landrieu was a good friend for parents in D.C. and cared about our children, which made her vote such a terrible disappointment."[81]

On September 4, 2003, the Senate Appropriations Committee approved $13 million for the program as part of their D.C. spending bill.[82] Two Democrats on the panel, Senators Dianne Feinstein and Robert C. Byrd, voted for the measure.

"I have begun to rethink public education, and I think we spend too much time supporting old structures and not enough time on what works for children," Feinstein said in a speech. "If we look at what works for children, we would probably agree that different models have to be provided, because what works for one child may not necessarily work for another."[83]

Meanwhile, Landrieu had shifted camps completely. By September 26, she railed on the floor of the Senate against the same proposal she had once sponsored.

"Although the proponents say they are interested in helping children in failing schools, the real issue for proponents of vouchers is they simply believe in choice. That, of course, is their prerogative. But to stand behind the visual of poor people struggling in schools that are failing is absolutely false," she said, proceeding to lecture against using parent satisfaction as a useful metric in evaluating education effectiveness. "If someone in this chamber has any way to measure parental happiness in a way that taxpayers could know if parents are a little happy, just a little happy, happy on Mondays and not on Fridays...please tell me because I would be open to discuss it."[84]

By One Vote

The very next day, the full House of Representatives started considering the D.C. spending bill that their appropriators had passed in July. Even though the appropriations bill included funding for the scholarships, the program itself still needed authorization, along with a process to administer the tuition assistance to families.

Representative Tom Davis introduced the crucial amendment that created the program. On September 9, our parents sat in the

House gallery with knots in our stomach, not knowing whether the Davis amendment would pass or fail. As the clerk opened the voting, we watched as Members of Congress slowly cast their votes. At times, we surged ahead, and at other times, we fell behind.

When the time for voting ended, we discovered that we had won by one vote—209 to 208.[85] Our group breathed a collective sigh of relief. Had just one of those "yes" votes switched to "no," our advocacy efforts that year would have come to naught. Instead, our proposal seemed very much alive. And despite the repeated efforts of Eleanor Holmes Norton to torpedo the spending bill because it included the scholarship program, the larger legislation passed in the House of Representatives the next day by a vote of 210 to 206.[86]

After the bill was passed, we went and thanked our supporters. We particularly wanted to thank Representative Harold Ford Jr., the lone Democrat in the House of Representatives who supported our program. He went against his party, and we knew that had taken a great deal of courage. He came out of his office to greet us, and I stepped forward to thank him for his courage to support our children. Before I could finish, he hugged me and said, "Sometimes, you just have to do what is right. I want to thank you for fighting."

14.
Threats and Contradictions

....

THE FASCINATING DEBATE ON CAPITOL Hill kept us on the edges of our seats. But at the same time, I was occasionally frightened by things that happened even closer to home.

In 2003, school choice for D.C. became the biggest news story in our area. The media wrote a lot about our efforts some positive stories, some neutral, and others fiercely negative.

One particularly scathing story in a local independent newspaper, the *Common Denominator*, published my home address after denigrating my character. Soon after, I began receiving death threats from scholarship opponents—including an especially vulgar and frightening call in the middle of the night. I also received death threats by mail, with people cutting out letters from newspapers and magazines to craft their hateful messages. Apparently, our opponents had watched too many bad movies.

The D.C. police started patrolling my street more often, too, after a car sat idling in front of my home for hours on end. I would be lying if I said that the threats did not frighten me. They did. They took me back to that cold winter night in 1967. This time, I didn't expect to see a burning cross on my small front yard, but I knew of the potential danger. But just like my Daddy before me, I did not back down.

To help navigate these media minefields, I knew I could always turn to a man named John Kramer, who worked at the Institute for Justice and helped train our parent leaders on effectively communicating with reporters. Whenever I found myself facing a public relations dilemma—like the situation with the *Common*

Denominator and so many others—John would remind me that just as the media could hurt our cause, they could help it by bringing to it public attention and support. "Keep telling your story," he would encourage me. "And don't let anyone stop you."

Unpleasantness also came from teachers' unions and their allies. Unfortunately, teachers' unions oppose all forms of school choice. They generally oppose open enrollment programs that allow students to go to traditional public schools outside of their geographic "zones." They generally oppose public charter schools, too. And they most definitely oppose opportunity scholarships. To them, keeping students in traditional public schools—where most teachers are often required to join unions—is simply a safer bet for their organizations' finances, regardless of whether the parents are satisfied or the students in these schools are succeeding.

As our army of parents fought for the opportunity scholarship proposal, teachers' unions and their allies lambasted us. In the summer of 2003, dozens of union-backed groups issued a steady stream of press releases deriding our proposal. To our delight, however, these organizations frequently contradicted each other.

On one hand, they claimed that D.C. did not need our scholarship program because "programs to improve student achievement in the District have been implemented [and] are working."[87] On the other hand, they painted a picture of a cash-starved, "debt-ridden" school system with "crumbling classroom ceilings" that needed millions of additional dollars so that it could improve and "showcase successful educational strategies."[88]

The contradictions didn't end there. These organizations could not decide amongst themselves whether our proposal was a bad idea because it *didn't serve enough* students or because it would serve *too many* students and therefore hurt D.C. schools' finances. "Current estimates show that only between 2,000 and 4,000 students…could benefit from the program," according to the American Civil Liberties Union (ACLU).[89] The People for the American Way said that the program was so small that it would only serve "a select few."[90] Another group, called Stop D.C. Vouchers, argued that this small program would "destroy" public education in D.C. by creating a "never-ending drain on public resources."[91]

These groups did not just oppose our efforts via press releases; their representatives harassed me at every chance they could.

At one evening meeting we held at a public housing project, a woman in the audience asked to speak. I recognized her from somewhere, but after thousands of meetings, I still couldn't place her or remember her name. After I invited her to stand and speak, she called me a fraud and told the crowd that I couldn't do anything to help them. She accused me of lying about how the scholarship program would benefit children and acted as a pawn of right-wing conservatives, attempting to brainwash anyone who listened to me. Suddenly, I remembered the woman's face: She worked for the nation's largest teachers' union in the U.S., the National Education Association.

Because she would not identify herself, I told the crowd who she represented. The entire audience started booing her for inserting herself in the meeting and for denigrating me. That night, thirty more parents signed up to go to Capitol Hill—to support the scholarship proposal—the following week.

I also started to get invitations to debate members of the teachers' unions about school choice. At these events, in addition to providing information about the legislation, I always told stories about how opportunity scholarships would help parents and their children. I refused to get into arguments with the opposing panelists who would personally attack me, using similar language that I had heard in that housing project meeting. Even though their words stung, I continued to provide the audience with information and introduce them to the children and parents who would benefit from this program by sharing their stories. Eventually, teachers' union representatives started telling members of the coalition that they didn't want to debate me. By refusing to take their negative bait, they claimed that I wasn't debating "fairly."

One Big Family

By the fall of 2003, most of our parent advocates had fought for their children's education and the creation of the scholarship program for years. Every single parent who had sacrificed time and made the effort to tell their stories and persuade the public and lawmakers about the benefits of school choice knew that their efforts would likely benefit *future children* even more than their own. To me, this selflessness sustained their engagement and our coalition.

Many of these parents came from low-income families, had not spent time in the public eye before this campaign, and until this point had never thought that their voices could matter. I prioritized building my relationships with them and nurturing them.

Every Thursday or Friday, I met with our parent leader group over lunch. We talked about our accomplishments and our future goals. We sorted out details and made assignments, but this meal together also let them know that I cared about them, wanted to hear their opinions and ideas, and worked to include them in discussions about our plans.

Almost every night, parents came over to my house for dinner. Even in the midst of a tension-filled legislative battle, we spent our days filled with joy. I felt as though my family had expanded, and my children felt the same way. I admit that I often behaved like my fellow parents' mama, hugging them and praising them and beaming all over when they did something wonderful. I expressed such affection not just because I knew that the success or failure of our efforts lay entirely with these powerfully motivated, committed, compassionate people. I did it because I loved them.

Storm Clouds

Even before our scholarship program passed in the House of

Representatives and cleared the Senate Appropriations Committee, we could see storm clouds on the horizon. Our old opponent, Senator Ted Kennedy, had announced in early September 2003 that he would work hand-in-glove with Eleanor Holmes Norton to defeat our proposal.

"Sen. Edward Kennedy plans to do everything he can to defeat the proposed use of school vouchers in the nation's capital," the Associated Press wrote on September 12, 2003. "Kennedy has said the voucher plan will take money from public schools and give it to private schools that do not have to meet as many testing and accountability requirements."[92]

News outlets also reported that Kennedy would filibuster the entire D.C. appropriations bill if he could not remove the scholarship program.[93] His threat worried us. We knew that Kennedy's reputation made him widely respected not only in the Democratic caucus, but by many of his Republican colleagues. If senators believed that he would carry through on his threat, we could lose a dozen or so supporters.

Working with our coalition partners, D.C. Parents for School Choice launched one of the most controversial advertising campaigns in the history of the school choice movement. The advertisement started with old newsreel footage of segregationist Alabama Gov. George Wallace literally standing in the schoolhouse door so that black children could not receive a public education. Then I appeared on the screen, asking Senator Kennedy how he could turn his back on black children today when his brothers—President John F. Kennedy and Senator Robert F. Kennedy—had fought so valiantly against the policies of the past that kept black students stuck in failing schools.

Even though we ran the ad only a few times, national news media quickly picked it up. Cable news networks played, and talked about, our ad again and again. Massachusetts reporters, in particular, wanted to interview me about the ad campaign—and I accepted every request.

"The Kennedy children have access to private schools," I told the *Springfield Republican* newspaper. "Our children did not. Not one Kennedy child had to worry about getting into good schools. Never, ever. We want to have the same resources."[94]

After viewing our ads, The *Boston Herald* excoriated Kennedy's position on our scholarship proposal, writing, "The parents of Washington, D.C., students are taking the fight for school vouchers to Sen. Ted Kennedy's back yard—that's right here—and well they should… The group will be running TV ads locally in an attempt to shame Kennedy into changing his mind…Shame, of course, only works on those with a conscience. And when it comes to his ideology vs. the needs of children in failing public schools, Kennedy apparently has no conscience—and no shame."[95]

One evening, as I was cooking dinner, my home telephone rang.

"Hello, this is Virginia," I answered.

"Virginia, this is Senator Ted Kennedy," said the man on the other end of the line.

I thought it was a hoax.

"Oh, no it's not, come on," I said.

"No, it really is," he insisted. "And I want to talk to you about that ad."

I could not believe that Senator Ted Kennedy had called me at home to talk about the ad. It seemed surreal, and yet, I also worried about what he would tell me. Had we alienated him forever?

"Your ads make me look like a racist," he said, "and I am not a racist. I want you to think about pulling that ad down."

"I understand, Senator," I replied. "But we are fighting for our children, and we will continue fighting for our children. The ad does not make you look racist. Your position on filibustering this legislation looks bad. I want you to reconsider."

"I will do that," he replied, "but please take that ad down."

What Senator Kennedy did not know—but I did—was that we did not intend to run the television ad more than a few times. Our advertising budget had run out. The earned media attention from the cable networks had given the ad a life of its own. In the end, the ad stopped running—because we never intended to run it anymore—and Kennedy eventually dropped his filibuster threat.

15.
At Long Last, Victory

....

WHEN SOME ELECTED OFFICIALS COMMIT to supporting a cause, they don't just lend their names to the effort. They put their heart, soul, and hard work into helping an idea come to life. Senator Dianne Feinstein proved herself as one of those leaders during our fight to create the opportunity scholarship program.

In response to Senator Kennedy's filibuster threat, Feinstein sprang into action, orchestrating several high-stakes and effective maneuvers to keep our opportunity scholarship proposal alive. For example, she invited D.C. Mayor Anthony A. Williams to stand next to her on the floor of the Senate in late September 2003 as she talked about the scholarship proposal's benefits.[96]

That conversation, as well as Williams' later comments at a press conference, proved riveting. As one reporter summed up, "Mayor Anthony A. Williams compared the failings of the District's public schools to a natural disaster Tuesday, urging the Senate to approve a federal school voucher program."[97] In response, Eleanor Holmes Norton smeared him as "a desperate man reaching for whatever he can say to avoid losing."[98]

But Williams' support alone didn't quell our concerns. In November, Democrats—including Landrieu—still wanted to remove the opportunity scholarship program from the D.C. appropriations bill. Talk of a filibuster still lingered in the air, and some congressional Republicans considered a last-minute removal of the program from the spending bill to speed its final passage.[99]

Finally, lawmakers decided to combine the D.C. spending bill, which had already passed in the House but remained stalled in the

Senate, into a much larger bill—one that would fund the entire federal government for 2004. This type of bill, called an omnibus appropriations bill, proved significantly harder to defeat, as failure to fund the federal government would mean an inevitable government shutdown.

On December 8, 2003, the House passed the 2004 omnibus bill by an overwhelming margin—with 244 Representatives voting in favor of the bill and 176 voting against it.[100] To help ensure that our program would remain in the Senate's version of the federal spending bill, Senators Judd Gregg and Mike DeWine worked to ensure that the Senate version would include provisions that would provide $1 to public schools and $1 to public charter schools for every $1 spent on scholarships—an effort strongly supported by Mayor Williams, School Board Chairwoman Peggy Cooper Cafritz, and Councilman Kevin P. Chavous.

Meanwhile, President Bush publicly pushed for the program's inclusion in government spending bills. In a White House speech to Catholic educators on January 9, 2004, the president said that private schools in D.C. provide "a really good alternative, and the federal government is now willing to help fund that alternative."

Finally, on January 22, 2004—after an attempted delay by Senator Landrieu—the Senate prepared to vote on the omnibus budget. Anything could have happened on the floor of the Senate— including an amendment to remove our program.

A Phone Call to Remember

I had long planned to have lunch with one of our supporters at Union Station in Washington, D.C., that day. I kept the appointment, knowing that after years of hard work, the decision to approve or deny the D.C. school choice proposal lay entirely in the hands of the Senate.

As I talked with my friend at Union Station that January day, a staff member from Senator Bill Frist's office called my cell phone to tell me that the Senate had passed the omnibus spending bill. Our $14 million program had survived the twists and turns of the legislative process and the changing political winds and would become law as part of an $820 billion federal spending bill.

I could hardly believe my ears. I thanked Senator Frist's staffer over and over again, hung up, and told my lunch companion that the legislation had passed. Both of us started jumping up and down, yelling our heads off, drawing stares and smiles from the diners around us.

The Washington Post summed it up nicely: "The Senate gave final approval to the nation's first federally funded school voucher program Thursday, ending nine years of acrimonious debate in Congress and sending $14 million a year in private school tuition grants to District of Columbia schoolchildren beginning this fall."[101]

In a very brief statement after the Senate's passage of the bill, President Bush singled out our program's inclusion in the budget. "I am pleased that the Senate has passed the omnibus budget bill, which fulfills important commitments like AIDS relief, education and D.C. school choice, veterans' health care, law enforcement, and other priorities," the president said.[102] On January 23, 2004, the president signed the bill, turning the D.C. School Choice Incentive Act of 2003 into a law of the land.

We felt genuine excitement and were full of energy. After all, we had spent years fighting for this proposal, exhausting ourselves in the process. To me, it seemed only fitting that I learned of the passage of the program by phone. After all, I first learned of the possibility of a scholarship program by chance—when I had answered that call from The Center for Education Reform seven years earlier.

Celebration
In the days following that vote, after President Bush signed the

bill, I gathered all our parents and children together for a huge pizza party. While the older children had stayed on the front lines with us throughout the campaign, we felt that the youngest children might not yet understand the reasons for our fight. While the older kids had become warriors and could talk about the fight with confidence, we thought that many of the younger kids might have just come along for the ride.

As we picked up the children and told them about the party, they were enthusiastic. When a pair of four-year-old twin boys saw me, they ran up to me and hugged me together. "Miss Virginia," they said. "Are we going to the Hill today to fight for our education?"

Their mother and I looked at each other, laughed, hugged them, and told them we were going to a party. Even at four years old, these twins understood that their mother, their friends' mothers, and I had fought for something important. We also knew that next year, when they started school, they would have the chance to go to a better school—and realize the benefits of all our incredible work.

Time to Spread the Opportunity

After President Bush signed the program into law, I felt confident that we had crafted a thorough program. The final legislation provided $7,500 scholarships to low-income children whose parents wanted to send them to private schools in the District, along with equal funding for traditional public schools and public charter schools. But the passage of a bill does not end the journey. Indeed, public policy is a marathon, not a sprint. We needed additional patience, diligence, and hard work to make sure that students could actually benefit from this new program.

I formed a partnership with the Washington Scholarship Fund to help with recruitment and the application process. Soon thereafter, I rejoiced when my sister Harrietta joined our team at D.C. Parents for School Choice, just as we shifted our focus to enrolling children in the program. Having Harrietta as a key member of our team—and having the "Fowler twins" working together again— was the perfect way to herald a new era in our work and lifelong partnership together, where we could work hand-in-hand to provide greater opportunities to children.

Together, we committed to visiting some of the most challenged communities where we knew families would qualify for the scholarship and having parents fill out applications on site. We considered this family outreach essential. After all, you can pass a law or create a program, but if you don't implement it appropriately, it won't serve as many families as it could.

Over time, we made the process even more efficient so that we could benefit as many children as possible. It became clear early on that families had difficulty getting photocopies and notary approval, so one of our team members became a notary public, and we bought a portable copy machine to eliminate those issues. We put everything in a big, black suitcase that rolled from neighborhood to neighborhood enrolling children in the program. It was a suitcase filled with hope.

As we expected, the program sparked high demand among low-income families. "Demand for access to the nation's first federally funded school voucher program has proved overwhelming in the nation's capital, due in large part to parental frustration with its troubled public education system," the Associated Press reported on June 11, 2004.[103]

But implementing a program effectively does not come easily. Before you can expect to get people to sign up for something, you need to educate them about what they're getting and help them make the best decision possible for their own children. As a result, over the four years of our outreach program—from 2004 to 2008—we conducted hundreds of small meetings in troubled areas of D.C., relying on a committed team of volunteers. We served crime-ridden areas of the city beset by drug activity, fighting, and violence.

I still believe that if our families have to live in troubled areas, then I will go to those areas to serve them. I have never been afraid. One night in one neighborhood, a drug dealer cautioned me that the scholarship application meeting needed to wrap up soon because it was getting dark and "when it gets dark, that's when my business begins."

He asked me why we had come to the neighborhood. I told him we wanted to sign kids up for a program that would allow them to go to better schools. He looked at me and finally responded, "You know what...take your time. If you are doing this for kids here, my business can wait." Later, he sent the mother of two of his children to sign up for the scholarship program, because he did not want his children to end up like him.

At another busy application meeting, I noticed a middle school-aged boy standing around and watching us. I thought he might be lost because he did not seem to have arrived at the meeting with a parent. I asked one of our volunteers to look into the situation and take care of the boy.

"Miss Virginia," the volunteer said, bringing the boy to me. "He is here alone. He wants to apply for a scholarship and fill out the form himself. He brought his school ID and a report card and wants to know if he can sign up."

I explained to the young man that he needed a parent to sign the scholarship forms.

"My mother is not around. She's a drug addict," he said. "I live with my grandmother, and she can't read. What should I do?"

Together, we walked to his house, talked his grandmother through the process, and helped them complete the application. As we left, the grandmother and her grandson were in tears—they now had a brighter future.

One father came to a scholarship application meeting we were conducting in one of the most violent communities in D.C. His disheveled appearance made us think that he had just wandered in, so I gently took his arm and attempted to lead him out. But he clearly—and loudly—stated that he wanted to apply for a scholarship for his son because he did not want his son to turn out like him. We worked with him for three days; every day we thought he might not return, but he did. On the final day, he still needed to provide one document. I told him I would pick it up at 9 a.m. When I arrived, I saw him sitting outside the building waiting in the rain. He had waited in the rain for several hours to make sure he didn't miss me.

One year later, during the scholarship renewal meeting, a man approached me, hugged me, and thanked me for helping him. Not recognizing him—he was neatly dressed and clean shaven—I accepted his thanks. Suddenly, I recognized him and could not believe his changed appearance. He told me that the success his son had experienced in his new, safe school made him want to do better also; he didn't want to embarrass his son. He was sober and working—and studying for his GED.

Another time, we had arranged for a meeting in a public housing project known for its crime and with many kids stuck in one of the worst schools in the city. As we approached, I saw lots of police near the building hosting the application meeting. I soon discovered that police were investigating a shooting that had occurred earlier. Right at that moment, one of the mothers who had organized the meeting came up to me. I told her I could reschedule, but she insisted that we have the meeting that evening because the parents she had spoken to were ready with all their documents. We couldn't get into the building, but we set up right out in front on the sidewalk and signed up fifteen families that evening. For these families, hope and opportunity couldn't wait—not one more day.

PART FOUR | *Saving School Choice*

16.

Elections Have Consequences

....

EVENTUALLY, OUR HARD WORK PAID off. As predicted, the D.C. Opportunity Scholarship Program proved to be not only proved popular but also incredibly effective. A federal study of the program indicated that families who used the scholarships felt more satisfied with their children's education than parents of public school students, and they also considered their children to be safer.[104]

The students themselves proved just as impressive as I could have hoped—demonstrating that when students receive better opportunities to learn and have high expectations, they meet and exceed those expectations. D.C. scholarship recipients graduated from high school at a rate of 91 percent, compared to just 70 percent for students in public-sector schools.

The program also had a profound impact on the quality of local public schools, especially for younger students. From the time the D.C. Opportunity Scholarship Program went into effect until 2015, "fourth-grade students made substantial gains relative to students in other large urban districts."[105] Charter schools in the District flourished, and the public school system embraced an open-enrollment model that created more choices and opportunities for families.

While they are still far from perfect—and still require significant improvements—public schools in the nation's capital today have made great strides since 1997, the year that I pulled William out of Roosevelt High School.

People of Color United

When political winds change, policies change too. In 2004, even as we celebrated the enactment of our scholarship program and started enrolling students, we knew that one election could upend all our hard work. Elections have consequences—for better and for worse.

For example, so many things changed for the better after Republican Win Rockefeller was elected Arkansas governor in 1967. He cleaned house, appointed a record number of black leaders to positions of power, and accelerated the process of school integration. And I will never forget how the election of George W. Bush in 2000 paved the way for the D.C. scholarship program's eventual passage.

And so, in 2004, I committed to doing everything I could to make sure that the man who had signed our program into law got re-elected. In August of that year, I created People of Color United to advocate for President Bush's second term.

Primarily comprised of radio ads that ran on black radio stations, People of Color United's campaign pointed out inconsistencies in John Kerry's record, asked what he had accomplished during his time in the Senate, and questioned the appropriateness of his wife describing herself—a white woman—as an "African American." Sure, the ads were hard-hitting, and at times tongue-in-cheek, but they represented my views. I wrote them. And I worked hard to raise money to fund them.

"I want people to think about how they're voting," I told the Knight Ridder Tribune News Service, "I think a lot of black people vote Democratic because that's how we always voted. I did for many years. I wanted people to think about the accomplishments of the administration and how it affects black people's lives."[106]

For even deigning to criticize the Democratic nominee and support a Republican, I was derided as someone who sought "voter suppression." To me, this attack was as racist as it was ludicrous.

The notion that trying to convince black voters to vote for a Republican amounted to voter suppression implies that black voters lack the intelligence to make their own choices.

"I was a Democrat for many, many years, and I want people to be informed voters," I explained on National Public Radio (NPR) amidst a barrage of criticism. "So, these ads were an attempt to get people talking about it—and certainly not to keep people out. To the contrary, [we wanted] to get people to inform themselves and to get all the information they could."[107]

In *Slate*, a left-leaning publication, one writer referred to our ad campaign as "The GOP Minstrel Show," concocted to "inflame gratuitous resentment of white people."[108] That made me laugh, because both men running for president were white—and I happened to support one of them. Perhaps my message that Democrats had taken black votes for granted had had an impact, since they reacted so angrily to the mere suggestion that black voters at least consider their options.

In November, President Bush surprised pundits by securing his re-election—and he did it in part by expanding his share of the black vote.[109] As a result, the D.C. Opportunity Scholarship Program continued to prosper—at least for the next few years.

Grandma

In case you think that school choice advocacy and politics consumed my entire life, let me assure you that they did not. In fact, some of my greatest memories from the mid-2000s came from my family.

In December of 2004, my daughter Miashia told me she was pregnant. She asked me to accompany her to childbirth classes—an experience that brought us even closer. I could not have felt more joy to spend this time with my daughter. Plus, Miashia was going to make me a grandmother!

On the afternoon of July 15, Miashia's husband called me and told me that Miashia's contractions had begun. I was immediately filled with excitement and anxiety. And just as my father had driven into a tree when he found out that my mother was pregnant with twins, Miashia's husband did something funny that evening. Instead of taking Miashia to the birthing center they had chosen in Maryland, he drove her to my house.

Together, we got Miashia to the birthing center, and early the next morning, she gave birth to a perfect little girl whom they named Yamundow. When the doctor placed tiny little Yamundow in my arms, we locked eyes, and I discovered a love that I didn't know I could summon for a person who was not my own child.

Two years later, my bond with Miashia and Yamundow was strengthened even more. Miashia and her husband divorced, and Miashia and my granddaughter moved back into my home. Harrietta and I loved having them with us. Later, after William completed his tour with the Marines, he too moved back in while he figured out the next steps in his career. Having two of my children, my sister, and my granddaughter under one roof with me was a great inspiration for me—especially as our D.C. school choice advocacy efforts kicked back into high gear.

In the years that followed, my personal blessings multiplied. Years before, my son Michael and his wife Nikki had moved to Dallas. So, I couldn't have been happier when in 2008, they welcomed their daughter—and another perfect granddaughter for me—Chloe into the world. In 2010, Nikki gave birth to their son and my first grandson, Jeremiah. And the family wasn't yet done! In 2015, they welcomed my third granddaughter, Genesis, into the world.

I have four perfect grandchildren and I love each of them with all my heart. And I take comfort in the fact that Miashia and Michael are not just good parents—they are amazing and compassionate caregivers.

2006 and 2008

If the 2004 election proved beneficial to the schoolchildren of Washington, D.C., the elections in 2006 and 2008 presented us with challenges.

In 2006, as Democrats took back control over the House of Representatives, early warnings signaled that some of the new Members of Congress wanted to eliminate the D.C. Opportunity Scholarship Program.

"Many families are beginning to worry that the change of power in Congress means the end of the scholarship program, and some parents say they're willing to fight to keep that from happening," *The Washington Times* reported.[110] We would indeed fight, and we found no shortage of allies willing to fight alongside us, including major newspaper editorial boards.

"This program gives low-income parents educational options, and it is operating successfully for scores of children," *The Washington Post* editorialized. "Opponents should think twice before they try to interrupt the education of these children."[111]

Thankfully, local leaders' support countered the opposition from some Democrats in Congress. Former Councilman Kevin P. Chavous and former mayor Anthony A. Williams forcefully advocated for the D.C. Opportunity Scholarship Program—convincing a majority of the Democrat-controlled D.C. City Council to sign a letter supporting the program's continuation.

In addition, the program expanded its base of local Democratic support. Former D.C. mayor Marion Barry—who had previously opposed our program—joined the chorus of support, writing in an opinion piece: "I know it may surprise some that I would support a school voucher program, but I am proud to do so—and I especially support the D.C. scholarships. Many here in Washington also favor this program: community and business leaders, educators, parents, and elected officials who are putting children first."[112]

In 2008, after Barack Obama was elected president, we knew

we needed to rebuild an even stronger parent army to save the program. During his campaign, then-Senator Obama signaled an openness to compromise on school choice.

"If there was any argument for vouchers, it was 'Alright, let's see if this experiment works,' and if it does, then whatever my preconceptions, my attitude is you do what works for the kids," he said. "I will not allow my predispositions to stand in the way of making sure that our kids can learn. We're losing several generations of kids, and something has to be done."[113]

In truth, Obama did become a strong supporter of public charter schools. I anticipate that his administration may eventually be viewed as a high-water mark for Democratic support for public sector school choice. But unfortunately, his campaign promises never extended to our scholarship program.

Immediately after taking office, the new president and Democratic majorities in Congress announced their intention to repeal, phase out, or scale back the program. "Democrats in Congress have put Washington, D.C., school officials on notice to prepare for the end of its voucher program," *Newsmax* reported on February 28, 2009.[114]

As we absorbed this news, I welcomed dozens of parents, tears streaming down their faces, to my home. How could a president who *looks like us* do this to us? they asked me. In our previous fight to pass the scholarship program, we became tenacious in our advocacy because we knew that school choice could bring the *potential* for greater opportunity. Now, the fight we had to wage—saving the D.C. Opportunity Scholarship Program—proved even more personal. If Congress did not reauthorize the program, thousands of students would have to leave their schools and return to the schools that their parents had specifically determined did not work for them.

Of course, the leaders who wanted to eliminate our program did not face the same worries that low-income D.C. parents did.

President Obama and his wife, First Lady Michelle Obama, chose the private Sidwell Friends School for their daughters, where they studied alongside opportunity scholarship recipients. Education Secretary Arne Duncan told a magazine that he refused to live in Washington, D.C. He instead settled in a Virginia suburb after moving from Chicago because "My family has given up so much so that I could have the opportunity to serve; I didn't want to try to save the country's children and our educational system and jeopardize my own children's education" by putting them in the D.C. public schools—the same schools that our students would return to if Congress eliminated the Opportunity Scholarship.[115]

But those commonsense arguments fell on deaf ears in Congress. In March, the Senate voted to strip the D.C. Opportunity Scholarship Program from the federal budget.[116] The omnibus spending bill signed by President Obama that same month reduced funding for the program, which would eventually have triggered its elimination.[117]

17.

Save the OSP

....

WITH THE IMMINENT ELIMINATION OF the D.C. Opportunity Scholarship Program at hand, our coalition of parents faced immediate urgency, and our broader advocacy army again kicked its efforts into high gear.

Kevin Chavous worked tirelessly on Capitol Hill to defend the program, raised funds to support the coalition's advocacy efforts, and served as a key media spokesperson. He also filmed a hard-hitting television ad taking aim at President Obama's position on the program. Together, Chavous and former mayor Anthony A. Williams wrote an op-ed in *The Washington Post* that attracted significant publicity.

"As a youth, Barack Obama benefited from educational scholarships," they wrote. "After college, he worked as a community organizer on behalf of low-income families in Chicago. Community organizer Obama would support those parents seeking better educational opportunities for their children. Community organizer Obama would embrace a program like the Opportunity Scholarships, which give the children of low-income parents a chance at the American dream—without having to wait five years for the local school reform plan to work."[118]

We benefited from the support of national organizations, notably the Alliance for School Choice and their president John Schilling, who worked tirelessly to coordinate federal lobbying for the program. The Heritage Foundation, the Friedman Foundation for Educational Choice, the Center for Education Reform, the Institute for Justice, the U.S. Conference of Catholic Bishops, and other organizations played important roles, too.

Each of these organizations brought their own unique talents, skills, and strategies to our fight. For example, our partners at the Heritage Foundation, Jennifer Marshall and Lindsey Burke—two extraordinarily talented and compassionate women—decided to launch a bus and billboard campaign, along with a special website that included videos of students from the scholarship program.

As part of the website, we told the parents that we wanted their children to write letters to President Obama about how they felt about their scholarships and schools—in their own words. Letter after letter came pouring in, filled with heartfelt stories asking the president to save their scholarships.

"Being a recipient of the opportunity scholarship has meant far more to me than can be quantified with words," wrote Jordan, a seventeen-year-old student. "This and other programs that allow choice in education have lifted children out of seemingly hope-less environments and have given them hopes and dreams of opportunities that have seemed far-fetched. I humbly ask that you continue funding programs that allow children a choice in their education."[119]

"Dear President Obama, I must first say congratulations on your victory…and becoming our first black president," wrote twelve-year-old Sakeithia. "My old public school was not a very safe place. I saw a lot of things a child should not see. I'm now learning things that were not offered to me in public school."[120]

We later videotaped students reading their letters at an annual school choice dinner our organization held for parents and children. One family arrived very late; when the mother and her two daughters walked in, the mom explained to me that her eldest daughter had run an extremely high fever all evening. The young girl insisted on coming to the taping because she wanted to save her scholarship.

Meanwhile, one of the people who provided so much advice and assistance, especially in helping communicate about the program's benefits to a national audience, was a 29-year-old staff member of the Alliance for School Choice named Andrew Campanella. Andrew became a close friend of mine—practically another son—and I later appointed him to serve as the only non-parent board member in the history of D.C. Parents for School Choice. From the minute the program was threatened in 2008 until the resolution of the battle in 2011, he came to my house at almost every chance he had.

As Andrew told the *Chicago Tribune* in March 2009, "It would be really shocking to see 1,700 kids removed from the best schools they have ever known."[121] Indeed, that issue defined our fight: to protect the educational futures of 1,700 children who had received scholarships and countless others who could benefit from the program in the future.

The program's parents helped to change hearts and minds. They never ceased to amaze me, and in the fight to save the scholarship program, our ranks swelled with young and enthusiastic parents eager to protect their children's educational futures—along with veterans of our initial advocacy battles in the late 1990s and early 2000s.

Parent Power

There's always one parent in the fight that organizers wish they could clone. And in our organization, that person was a mother named Patricia. She epitomized our fight to reauthorize opportunity scholarships. She never said no to a request to support the program that had given her two sons a better chance in life. One day, Patricia and her sons agreed to participate in a particularly time-intensive project. They agreed to film personal videos for *every single* undecided or on-the-fence Member of Congress, as well as thank you videos for key supporters. When I arrived at the office to tape the ads, I looked at Patricia and instantly knew that something was wrong. One of the videographers pulled me aside and said, "Miss Virginia, Patricia's mom died last night. She said she didn't tell you because you would have told her not to come today, and she didn't want to let you or this program down." I gave Patricia and her sons a giant hug. After they filmed their videos, they went home to make funeral arrangements.

Two other parents also served as heroes of our reauthorization fight: A father named Joe and a mother named Sheila. Joe had four children, all of them adopted, and worked tirelessly to give them a better chance at success. From attending and speaking at rallies to painting signs, Joe and his children provided encouragement and support to so many other parents who had never before advocated for school choice in such a high-stakes battle.

Sheila had one daughter, Shawnee, and brought a sense of peace, calm, and determination to every meeting she attended. We became dear friends, and Sheila later served on the board of the organization that administered the scholarship program. Shawnee graduated as the valedictorian of the private high school that she attended—a proud recipient of a D.C. Opportunity Scholarship.

During the fight to save the program, we didn't face many difficulties generating public support—because almost everyone saw its impact. When D.C. Parents for School Choice announced an effort to gather local signatures on a petition to save the program, we garnered 7,400 signatures in a very short period of time.

When we planned a massive rally on D.C.'s Freedom Plaza on May 6, 2009, more than 1,000 children and parents filled the plaza, all wearing "Put Kids First" T-shirts and holding colorful, hand-painted signs and banners. As one of the moms attending the rally, Ingrid Campbell, told Reason Television, "I thought it was going to be a couple of people...talking and speaking amongst each other. No, this turned out to be bigger than we thought it was going to be."[122] The rally proved an enormous success, generating significant attention in the local and national press.

"This program has worked well. It has been successful for the schools, for the parents, and more importantly, for the children." said Kevin Chavous at the event. "Right now, some folks in Congress want to end this program, but we're not going to accept that, are we? We're sending the message that every child matters."[123]

"The whole world is watching Washington, D.C.," said Ben Chavis, former executive director of the NAACP and a school choice advocate. "Every parent should have the right of choice. Every parent should be able to choose the best school for their children."[124]

"I refuse, refuse, refuse to be someone's inmate or charity case, and I'm putting all the disbelievers in their place," said Carlos Battle, a high school student who had received an opportunity scholarship, as he read his poem, "Surrender Me." "I'm not going to be thrown in the category of jailed or shot, I'm the new face of black youth—like it or not."[125]

When the rally concluded, I led hundreds of parents and students in a march to the office of D.C. Mayor Adrian Fenty, who had not yet endorsed our program. Together, we carried backpacks filled with the 7,400 signatures. "These are the voices of D.C. residents," I said. "These are his constituents."[126]

As Mary Katharine Ham noted in *The Washington Examiner*, many of the attendees at our Freedom Plaza rally were "single parents who had to get off work" to attend the event.[127] To my memory, this article—written more than eleven years after we first started fighting for school choice in Washington, D.C.—marked the first time that anyone in the media noted the sacrifices that so many of our parents had made, on a daily basis, to support the program.

Glimmers of Hope
The day after our Freedom Plaza rally, the Obama Administration

leaked news that the president would allow students who were currently receiving scholarships to remain in the program.[128] However, that decision led to more questions than answers. Specifically, this "compromise" proposal would mean rescinding scholarships that had been awarded to 216 D.C. students the year before and preventing new students from entering the program.

The revocation of scholarships from 216 students became not just a faraway policy challenge to overcome—nor "save the 216" simply a rallying cry. These children included the sons and daughters of parents I knew and loved—people who came to my house regularly for lunch and dinner with Harrietta and me. These people had become part of our extended family. To see them feel hopeless—just as I had when William lacked good options for his schooling—saddened and infuriated me. If rescinding the scholarships sought to divide our parent group and to dampen the optimism of families who had fought for their children's education, it had the opposite effect. These parents were mad—and spoiling for a fight.

Days later, Senator Joe Lieberman held a hearing in his Senate committee about the program, featuring only glowing endorsements from students, parents, and local leaders. Lieberman had invited scholarship opponents, but they refused to attend and have their voices heard in public. Instead, they chose to work behind closed doors.[129] But dozens of parents of those 216 students sat in that hearing room. Even though their children's scholarships had been revoked, they determined to still speak out.

Later that summer, a group of education reform and school choice organizations commissioned a public poll of D.C. residents. The results confirmed what we already knew: our program remained wildly popular. "Nearly 75 percent of respondents said they 'somewhat' or 'strongly' favor the scholarship program," the poll indicated. "Eighty-two percent of parents of school-age children favor the program."[130]

Of course, no legislative battle can succeed without committed legislators. Our original legislative champions not only stuck with us, they stuck out their necks to keep our program alive. In addition to Senator Joe Lieberman—who *The Washington Post* called "the Senate's most outspoken supporter of the D.C. voucher initiative," Senator Susan Collins and Representative John Boehner carried the flag for the program on Capitol Hill.

Meanwhile, elected officials who opposed our program, including Senator Dick Durbin and Representative Jose Serrano, found themselves on the receiving end of our hard-hitting newspaper ads in their home states and districts. So did D.C. Delegate Eleanor Holmes Norton, who sparred with us on a near-daily basis.

Just like our first fight to create the D.C. Opportunity Scholarship Program, we refused to pull punches when elected officials threatened the futures of children and families in our program. For Members of Congress, a negative newspaper advertisement might have some political consequences. But for the students who received scholarships to attend the schools of their parents' choice, ending or curtailing the program could have had lifelong repercussions. We would do practically anything to prevent that.

18.

A Long, Hot Summer

....

FOR WEEKS IN JULY AND August of 2009, students and parents who had benefited from the scholarship program sat outside the U.S. Department of Education, holding a daily silent protest against the Obama administration's position on the program. We carried signs, sat under trees for shade, guzzled bottles of water, and tried our best to keep our spirits high. Parents also shared their experiences with the news media.

"This program means everything," said Patricia William. "[My son] was in public school and it didn't work for him. He experienced a lot of difficulty. Not to speak badly about public school, but he suffered. Public schools are not meant for every child. People have different needs."[131]

Washington's brutal summer heat scorched us, and from time to time, a man aligned with the teacher's unions interrupted our silent protest. He parked his air-conditioned car right next to the students and parents, using a high-volume bullhorn with two loudspeakers to scream at the children. In response, we sang songs and chanted positive messages.

Civil Disobedience

In September, we escalated our protests. I linked arms—literally—with other black leaders, including Dr. Howard Fuller, Kevin Chavous, former Black Alliance for Educational Options president Gerard Robinson, and North Carolina education reform leader Darrell Allison for a show of civil disobedience at the Department of Education. We wanted to form a human chain and block the doors of the Department, just as the administration wanted to block the doors of opportunity for the children in our program and other families who would benefit from it.

This time, we all but knew we would face arrest. We had lawyers on hand to handle bail and pastors to pray for us. In the weeks before this dramatic act, I met with some of the parents of opportunity scholarship recipients in my home. Almost ever person wanted to join the protest, link arms with us, and risk their own arrest.

"I will do anything for this program and for my kids," Joe Kelley told me.

"Same here," said Patricia William. "There is nothing I will not do. This is too important."

But I knew that putting parents—especially black and brown moms and dads—at risk of arrest had its drawbacks. For me, an arrest wouldn't affect my advocacy work in the slightest. But for a mother or father who faced many of the same struggles in life that I had just a decade before, an arrest and criminal record could have dashed their career plans. No symbolic gesture was worth putting the students we wanted to help, and the parents we hoped to empower, in harm's way. Thankfully, the parents understood. But they did show up—hundreds of them—and marched with us to the door of the U.S. Department of Education with tears in their eyes.

We later learned that the administration had told police not to make any arrests that day. After standing nose-to-nose with the police for quite a while—with hundreds of students and parents cheering us on—we left and addressed the media.

"As a product himself of private school scholarships, the president's actions are bizarre and misguided," I said. "The bottom line is that it is morally wrong to block low-income children from attending great schools, and this Administration knows it."[132]

After that event, Kevin Chavous gave one of the most powerful speeches I had ever heard—a speech that he hadn't even written or prepared, because we all expected to be thrown in a paddy wagon and taken to jail.

"Each and every child is entitled to equal access to the American Dream. Each and every child is entitled to a high-quality education. And it is shameful if we give them anything less," he said. "That is the last civil-rights challenge for our country. That is why I stand here. That's why those of us who are here before you dedicate our lives to this cause. That's why you don't have to arrest us, because we ain't going nowhere."[133]

A Historic Rally

Even with our almost daily sit-ins at the Department of Education offices and our other acts of civil disobedience, we needed to do even more to maintain the pressure on Congress and President Obama to save the program that had made such a positive difference in thousands of students' lives.

Working with the Alliance for School Choice, the Institute for Justice, the Friedman Foundation for Educational Choice, The Center for Education Reform, and other partners, D.C. Parents for School Choice set out to achieve an ambitious goal—planning the largest school choice rally in D.C. history.

Planning such a big event, especially one including thousands of students and parents, takes time and effort. Getting permits alone involves wrangling bureaucratic processes. Setting up staging and speaker systems, distributing T-shirts, and organizing boxed lunches takes even more time.

Logistics for the big day became one of the most time-consuming parts of our rally. We knew that for our event to make a difference, we needed authentic homemade signs, and we wanted parents and their children to make them. Harrietta and I bought markers, paint, and crayons. For weeks, we invited parents and their children to our Hawaii Avenue house to paint those signs.

My little granddaughter Yamundow helped, and our big and

loveable dog, Bo, kept us company by sleeping on some of our newly painted signs. Despite the high stakes and the uphill battle we faced, those days and nights spent painting and drawing and cooking hamburgers and catfish for the families of the D.C. Opportunity Scholarship remain among my fondest memories.

Finally, with all our permits secured, logistical plans in place, and signs painted, the day of the rally arrived. On September 30, 2009, thousands of D.C. Opportunity Scholarship Program supporters gathered in Upper Senate Park for the "Save School Choice" rally. While the sight of thousands of people clad in yellow "Put Kids First" T-shirts energized me, nothing inspired me more than hearing from the students and parents who spoke that day.

"I would not be standing before you if it wasn't for the Opportunity Scholarship Program," said Ronald Holassie, a junior at Archbishop Carroll High School, the school William had attended back in the 1990s. "I have evolved into the young man who stands before you now. This is what the program has made of me and others: a success."[134]

"I want to share my experience with you. I am so proud every day to wake up in the morning and see the smile, and drop these kids off to school at a safe environment," said Ronald's mother, Carmen.[135]

One mother, LaTasha, talked about her two children: "We want to tell the president and congressmen to put kids first. I'm a parent of two children—a single parent—and one of them is one of the 216 [students] that [Education Secretary Arne] Duncan had the audacity to slap in the face and take back the scholarships that he gave us. We won't tolerate that, will we?"[136]

Dr. Howard Fuller—the man to whom I had originally turned years before to learn about advocacy, and the man whom I had linked arms with the month before—issued a forceful demand to our nation's leaders.

"We're here to tell the president, and Arne Duncan, and the

Congress, that our children are our most precious gift from God and that it is our responsibility, with God's guidance, to love them, to nurture them, to care for them—and to make sure every single one of [them] is educated," said Dr. Fuller.[137]

In addition to a host of other supporters, House Minority Leader John Boehner attended and spoke. In a private moment before he stepped up on stage, he pulled me aside. "Keep up what you're doing," he said. "This matters. These students matter. We can't let them down."

By October, our daily campaign—from sit-ins to protests to silent marches to rallies—began to have an impact. Robert Tomsho reported in *The Wall Street Journal* that "after months of pro-voucher rallies, a television-advertising campaign and statements of support by local political leaders, backers say they are more confident about its prospects. Even some Democrats, many of whom have opposed voucher efforts, have been supportive."[138]

Unfortunately, events occurred that dashed our hopes. As Bill Dupray wrote in *The Washington Examiner* on December 30, 2009, "House and Senate appropriators this week...have mandated the slow death of the D.C. Opportunity Scholarship Program...The decision to end the program, a decision buried in a thousand-page spending bill and announced right before the holidays, destroys the hopes and dreams of thousands of D.C. families."

The decision meant that while students who had already been given scholarships could keep them, no new students could enter the program. For a year, we kept up our protests and activism; however, barring a major breakthrough, our program likely would not survive.

Luck Strikes Again

Luck has a way of striking twice. In my case, luck seems to strike at the right moments—including in November 2010. When Republicans took control of the House in a massive political realignment in the midterm elections, our lead supporter in the House of Representatives, Representative John Boehner, became Speaker of the House.

As one of his first acts as Speaker, Boehner invited President Obama to deliver his State of the Union Address to Congress on the evening of January 25, 2011. Days before the president's speech, Boehner had reached out to me through his aide, Katherine Haley.

The new speaker had a plan. Instead of inviting adults to sit in the coveted seats of the Speaker's box in the House chamber to watch President Obama deliver his State of the Union, he would fill those seats with D.C. Opportunity Scholarship recipients, teachers, and some of our key supporters. Katherine explained that Boehner wanted to make sure that if President Obama glanced up from his podium, he would have to look these students in the eye.

The move worked brilliantly—and thrilled our students and supporters. Despite our frustrations with President Obama, our young students found attending a State of the Union speech fascinating and educational. When we arrived at the Capitol, Speaker Boehner greeted each student by name, talked about how much he cared about their future, and even shed a few tears. After we all enjoyed some food, Boehner took us on a tour of the Capitol, including his private balcony.

As we filed into the House gallery and took our seats in Boehner's box, we couldn't believe that of all the major national priorities on Boehner's plate, he had taken the time to recognize the plight of our program.

The next day, Boehner's office told *Politico* that he indeed viewed the preservation of our program as a top priority and planned to introduce legislation to reauthorize it.

"The D.C. vouchers funding could be the only bill Boehner authors all year, his office said," reported *Politico*, noting that the speaker would personally author this bill "to stress how important he views the program, and he is not co-sponsoring any [other][139] legislation this Congress."

Days later, Boehner and Lieberman introduced the Scholarships for Opportunity and Results (SOAR) Act.

On March 30, the House of Representatives passed the bill by a vote of 225-195. As Members of Congress voted, D.C. students and parents filled a congressional meeting room just steps away from the House chamber. Each of these families stood up at a microphone and told their stories. Then, Kevin Chavous and I led the crowd in a rare indoor rally.

After Members of Congress voted, we invited each of them to speak at a "rolling press conference," which lasted several hours. Still, the vote seemed largely symbolic because the Boehner reauthorization bill would likely be "dead on arrival" in the Senate, despite the vigorous support of Senators Lieberman, Feinstein, Collins, and others. Or, so we thought.

19.
New Beginnings

....

JUST A WEEK AFTER THE press conference on Capitol Hill,
everything changed. Nothing short of a lightning bolt of jubila-
tion replaced our pessimism about the Senate stalling on Speaker
Boehner's bill to reauthorize the D.C. Opportunity Scholarship
Program.

During the previous month, President Obama and Speaker
Boehner had engaged in tense negotiations over the federal
budget. Funding for the entire government would run out at the
stroke of midnight on Saturday, April 9, 2011. Several attempts to
resolve their disagreements had failed, and the U.S. government
was careening towards another shutdown.

Late on the evening of Friday, April 8, 2011—just one hour
before the federal government would close due to the funding
lapse—a breaking news alert appeared on my phone: Speaker
and President Obama had reached a budget deal. Sitting in bed,
I searched the internet for information about the program. But I
found nothing.

Finally, I received a text message from Katherine Haley. Lawmakers had included the D.C. Opportunity Scholarship Program,
and Speaker Boehner's bill to save and expand it, in the spending
bill. As one of Speaker John Boehner's must-have priorities, he
had demanded its inclusion as he and the president finalized their
spending agreement.

Passing the Torch
With the scholarship program saved and educational opportunities

for D.C. parents preserved, I knew in my heart that I had to make some tough choices of my own.

I had just turned sixty years old. Fourteen years of rallying, marching, and organizing had taken its toll. While my mental spirit remained strong, my body ached. Pounding the pavement at rallies, walking to Capitol Hill, and canvassing neighborhoods had done a number on my knees. It was becoming physically tougher for me to move around and get places.

Also, as previously mentioned, I had become a grandmother. I had watched mothers and fathers half my age—passionate, drive, and motivated to do the right thing—work alongside me in the fight to reauthorize the D.C. Opportunity Scholarship Program. Had the time come to pass the torch of school choice advocacy—in Washington, D.C., at least—to this next generation? I prayed for clarity, but I already knew the answer to that in my heart.

I had also become an empty nester once again. Harrietta had moved back to our hometown of Little Rock in 2009. Daddy had died in 1985, and Mama was not getting any younger. Harrietta understandably wanted to spend quality time with the woman who had given us girls such encouragement and inspiration. Miashia and Yamundow had also moved to their own homes, as had William.

With an empty house but a full heart, I felt the pull of Little Rock calling me back home. I missed Mama, too. But D.C. had always acted as a magnet, keeping me close. Moving would mean saying farewell to the parents who had become my extended family for so many years. It would mean bringing this definitive chapter of my life—working to create, promote, and save our scholarship program—to an end.

One morning, as I sat with my coffee at the same kitchen table where we had made so many plans, painted so many signs, and sorted so many petitions, I found the answer. Yes, it was time to go home.

My house had emptied, and my children had grown—on their own, and with their own children. The families of the D.C. Opportunity Scholarship Program had continued their own lives, their children happier in their new schools. I knew then that while the fight for school choice will never end, my work in this city had come to a close. There is a season in life for everything, and the sun had set on one season for me—hopefully to rise once again for another.

I would go back to where it all started: Little Rock, Arkansas. I would take some time off to spend with my family, enjoy my mother's sunset years, and think about what the future held.

When I told the families I had worked with for years of my decision, they expressed sadness about my departure. But they understood. So did our advocacy partners. For one final send-off, they all joined together to throw me a giant going-away celebration at the U.S. Capitol. Watching the parents of our program sit at dinner tables next to Speaker Boehner, Senator Lieberman, and countless other national leaders put the battles over the past fourteen years into perspective. Finally, D.C. parents truly had a seat at the table, and lawmakers were listening to them. I couldn't have asked for a better farewell gift.

Packing Up and Saying Goodbye

For fourteen years, my rowhouse on Hawaii Avenue had served as the *de facto* headquarters for the D.C. parent movement for school choice. For fourteen years before that, it had functioned as the home in which I raised my children. In principle, moving sounded freeing. But packing up the house was a different story.

Throughout all my years of working in school choice and asking some of the biggest charitable foundations and wealthiest individuals to support our cause, I had never earned much money from my advocacy work. Whenever people donated to our organization, I put that money to the cause—and I paid myself very little. I had never sought to profit off of our advocacy; I thought that would betray the families we were serving and the donors who were contributing to our work. Looking back, though, I wished I had put some money aside for retirement.

My lack of savings had made moving back home a do-it-yourself project. I called some of my closest friends—Joe Kelley, Patricia William, Sheila Jackson, and Andrew Campanella. Together, they joined William, Miashia, and me in packing up the house so that another group of friends could drive a moving truck from D.C. to Arkansas.

In every corner of my home, we discovered artifacts from school choice fights gone by. One closet contained rally signs from our first advocacy work in the late 1990s. Another drawer contained paints and markers we had to make signs for other events. We found copies of our petitions, brochures, and more than enough of our white D.C. Parents for School Choice T-shirts, along with yellow shirts from our reauthorization fight.

Packing was a chore, but that rowhouse on Hawaii Avenue had truly seen a lot. So much good had come from our work together. All of those artifacts gathering dust had helped bring a big, bold, aspirational idea to life for thousands of children.

Moving into a house right next to Mama with my sister in Little Rock, I knew I couldn't keep it all. We couldn't fit much into our small new home. "Everyone, take what you want," I told my dear friends who helped me move. "Keep some of these memories for yourself."

Finally, we packed the truck. I hugged my friends and slept that night alone in an empty house. The next morning, as I prepared to leave for the long drive back to Arkansas, I invited some of those same friends over for coffee. All that remained in the kitchen was a coffeemaker and a table. As we sat around, talked, and cried, the empty house echoed. No longer the headquarters of a parent movement, no longer a home, it had become just another row-house on Hawaii Avenue.

My friends eventually left, and I said goodbye to the house. Then, I got in my car and headed south. I cried, reflecting on the thirty-four years I had spent in the District of Columbia. Had I left behind unfinished business? No, I thought, I had done my part—tiny though it may seem in the giant kaleidoscope of life.

For my own children, I would have done anything to give them opportunities in life—the same opportunities my parents and ancestors had struggled to give our family. When I saw injustice, I had fought against it—just like Mama and Daddy had done decades before. When I saw doors closed to me or to others because of our race or income, I had joined with other parents to open those doors and encourage children to run through them and seize opportunities.

And through it all, I had stayed true to the principles that my parents had taught me—chief among them, the importance of kindness, compassion, and love. For if they taught me one thing that I will never forget, it was this: To open minds, to open doors, and to make change, you must first open hearts. As I headed back to where it all began—Little Rock—I didn't know what my future held. But I knew that if I had helped open just a few hearts of my own, the legacy my family had entrusted with me would indeed carry on.

Afterword

On May 7, 2018, I stood in the audience at a school choice rally on Capitol Hill—right near the spot where we had held our historic 2011 rally to save the D.C. Opportunity Scholarship Program. I looked at a crowd filled with people wearing yellow shirts that read "Save the Kids" and holding handmade signs.

On the stage, a strong black woman introduced herself to the crowd as Virginia Walden. The crowd roared—as did I.

The woman was an actress—the talented, Emmy-winning Uzo Aduba. Even though I had never made much money from my advocacy work on behalf of school choice, and had rarely sought credit for it, Hollywood had taken note of my improbable story. The journey of a single mom who worked with other parents to change federal law and provide children with greater educational opportunities sounded promising to producers. As a result, the producers cast Uzo to play me in *Miss Virginia*, a film inspired by our story.

I cannot describe what it feels like to have a movie made about our work. Indeed, the honor humbles me, not least because Uzo Aduba captures my spirit perfectly. But truthfully, the film also scares me. I worry how people—from family, to friends, to fellow advocates, to total strangers—will react to it, especially since it proved challenging for the filmmakers to condense fourteen years of advocacy efforts into less than two hours. The film certainly takes some creative liberties, changing some names, omitting some details, and condensing some experiences. But it accurately depicts the passion with which D.C. parents fought for their children's futures.

Most importantly, I hope that the film inspires parents. I hope that it shows parents the power of their stories and experiences and the importance of standing up and fighting for what is right. I hope it convinces more families to do what it takes to open doors and open hearts.

Honestly, even though I will remain steadfast in my support for school choice, I do worry about the future of the school choice movement. I worry mainly because it has become incredibly difficult for genuine, authentic parent groups to form and flourish in communities across the country.

Times have changed. Communication via Twitter has, for some people, replaced the person-to-person and door-to-door advocacy that defined our campaigns in the District of Columbia. Regardless of advances in social media and technology, there will always be power in convening people by bringing them together in one room.

Parents must also reassert their roles as leaders of this movement. A greater number of national organizations support school choice than ever before. Parents have key roles to play in these groups—not just as tokens occasionally called to speak on conference panels, but as leaders and organizers. To grow and expand, the school choice movement must not become bureaucratized.

Finally, people everywhere need to learn to work with each other. Our country has become plagued by a crisis of division. Only by working together can we bridge these gaps. I certainly did not agree with the political views of all the parents who fought alongside me for school choice in Washington, D.C. I did not agree with all of the political positions of our congressional allies. But we worked together because, rather than emphasizing our differences, we focused on the goals that united us.

Regardless of your path on your own school choice journey,

please know that I will always stand with you, ready to help in whatever way I can. While I may have passed my torch, as long as doors and hearts remain to be opened, I will remain in this fight. I will keep the legacy.

Virginia Walden Ford
August 5, 2019
Little Rock, Arkansas

Acknowledgements

....

I AM FILLED WITH GRATITUDE for the many inspirational, loving, compassionate, and pioneering people who made my life's journey possible.

Without question, I will remain forever grateful for my parents, William Harry Fowler and Marion Virginia Fowler Armstrong. In so many ways, they passed to me a legacy that I have worked to keep, in my own way.

To my sisters Gail, Doris, and Renee; and to beloved twin, Harrietta: I am grateful to each of you for different things, but my love for you is stronger than you know.

My children have been the light of my life, and my grandchildren make those lights shine even brighter. To my children Michael, Miashia, and William and to my daughter-in-love, Nikki, I would walk to the ends of the earth for you, and I know you would do the same for me. To my grandchildren Yamundow, Chloe, Jeremiah, and Genesis, I cannot begin to tell you how proud I am to be your grandma. The torch is now passed to each of you; I hope you will run with it and keep our family's legacy in your own ways, too.

To each and every person who was involved in the fight to create, protect, restore, and expand the D.C. Opportunity Scholarship Program, "thank you" seems too quaint and insufficient a term. All of you—and most especially, the parents who made D.C. Parents for School Choice the force that it was—are heroes. There are too many of you to list by name, and I would require another book filled with gratitude to do so.

Writing a memoir is an interesting experience. While it provided a unique trip down memory lane, I will be honest in that I much preferred the day-to-day activities of fighting for school choice. Several people were enormously helpful in this process. Among them were my incomparable friend and colleague, Katie Parsons, whose support for me and my work extends beyond her contributions to this project. Megan Trank from Beaufort Books has been a true blessing, as well. And to my dear "son," Andrew Campanella, my sincere, heartfelt thanks for all you do now and in the past. Your friendship and support have exceeded so many boundaries that it would take a lifetime plus to thank you.

My journey has been one of love, hope, joy and faith. Everyone I've been so privileged to touch has made it an adventure that will stay with me forever. I love you all!

About the Author

....

Virginia Walden Ford is one of America's leading advocates for parent empowerment. As a student, mother, advocate, and grandmother, she has spent her lifetime fighting to create new educational opportunities for children and families. A native of Little Rock, Arkansas and the daughter of two public school educators, Virginia and her twin sister, Harrietta, were among the second wave of students chosen to desegregate Little Rock Central High School in the mid-1960s.

While she was raising her three children in Washington, D.C., Virginia created D.C. Parents for School Choice and built an army of parents to successfully advocate for the passage of the D.C. Opportunity Scholarship Program. This dramatic seven-year fight, and Virginia's role in it, was the inspiration for the feature film, *Miss Virginia*, starring starring Uzo Aduba, Matthew Modine, Amirah Vann, Vanessa Williams and Niles Fitch.

Today, Virginia lives, once again, in Little Rock, Arkansas. She travels the country speaking to parents and education groups, encouraging moms and dads and grandparents to discover the value of their voices and the importance of their advocacy.

Virginia is the proud mother of Michael Walden (and mother-in-law to Nikki Walden), of Miashia Walden Gaye, and of William Walden; she is the proud grandmother to Yamundow Virginia, Chloe, Jeremiah, and Genesis.

Endnotes

1   Associated Press, "Negro Educator Picks Little Rock Teachers," *Green Bay Press-Gazette*, February 9, 1967.

2   Associated Press, "Negro Gets Little Rock School Post," *Quad-City Times*, February 9, 1967.

3   Associated Press, "Little Rock Negro Takes School Post," *The Philadelphia Inquirer*, February 9, 1967.

4   Associated Press, "Negro Sees Little Difficulty in Teacher Hiring Assignment, *Northwest Arkansas Times*, February 9, 1967.

5   Ibid.

6   Ibid.

7   Ibid.

8   Information about my great-great grandfather, Nathan Warren, is derived from a variety of sources, including family history and legend, newspaper clippings from the 1800s, and Margaret Smith Ross's profile of Warren in the Spring 1956 edition of *The Arkansas Historical Quarterly*, titled, *"Nathan Warren: A Free Negro in the Old South."*

9   "Proceedings of the Convention of Colored Citizens of the State of Arkansas: Held in Little Rock, Thursday, Friday, and Saturday, November 30, December 1 and 2," Colored Conventions, http://coloredconventions.org/items/show/559.

10   Encyclopedia of Arkansas, "Ku Klux Klan (after 1900)," Encyclopedia of Arkansas, March 16, 2018, https://encyclopediaofarkansas.net/entries/ku-klux-klan-2755/.

11   Associated Press, "Bomb Shakes Pupil's Home in Little Rock," *The Bridgeport Post*, February 10, 1960.

12   Associated Press, "Gov. Faubus Comes from Deep in Hill Country and He Seldom Goes All-Out in Any Direction," *Chicago Tribune*, September 5, 1967.

13   Ibid.

14 Ibid.

15 UPI, "Winthrop Rockefeller Takes on Faubus Again," *The Ogden Standard-Examiner*, January 11, 1966.

16 Cathy Kunzinger Urwin, "'Noblesse Oblige' and Practical Politics: Winthrop Rockefeller and the Civil Rights Movement," *The Arkansas Historical Quarterly*, Spring 1995, Vol. 54, No. 1.

17 "8 States that Hold the Key to '68," *Fort Lauderdale News*, November 6, 1966.

18 "Elections to Watch," *The Daily Courier*, November 2, 1966.

19 Associated Press, "Rockefeller, Johnson Battle Down to Line in Rough Race," *The Shreveport Times*, November 6, 1966.

20 Ibid.

21 Richard Harwood, "Jim Johnson Trails Winthrop Rockefeller," *The Washington Post*, November 7, 1966.

22 Ibid.

23 Ibid.

24 Ibid.

25 Associated Press, "Rockefeller Wins Governorship," *Northwest Arkansas Times*, November 9, 1966.

26 John R. Starr, "Rocky Wins," *Associated Press*, November 9, 1966.

27 Associated Press, "5,000 Pay King Tribute in Little Rock," *The Shreveport Times*, April 8, 1968.

28 Editorial, "With His Box of Matches," *The Rayne Acadian-Tribune*, April 4, 1968.

29 Editorial, "Trigger To Bloody Confrontation," *The Delta Democrat-Times*, April 3, 1968.

30 Adrienne T. Washington, "Smith's Critics Merit Large Share of Blame," *The Washington Times*, June 2, 1995.

31 James F. Hirni, "Making the Worst Out of D.C. Schools," *The Washington Times*, November 1, 1995.

32 Tamara Henry, "D.C. Takeover Expected," *USA Today*, November 14, 1996.

33 Jerry Gray, "House Approved School Voucher Plan for Nation's Capital," *The New York Times*, October 10, 1997, https://www.nytimes.

com/1997/10/10/us/house-approves-school-voucher-plan-for-nation-s-capital.html.

34 New York Times News Service, "House Approves School Voucher Test Program," *The News and Record*, October 9, 1997, https://www.greensboro.com/house-approves-school-voucher-test-program/article_ebc42916-a126-5df8-9681-81abfde85acc.html.

35 Bruce Alpert, "Loud and Clear – People Politics and Policy," *The Times-Picayune*, September 21, 1997.

36 New York Times News Service, "House Approves School Voucher Test Program," *The News and Record*, October 9, 1997, https://www.greensboro.com/house-approves-school-voucher-test-program/article_ebc42916-a126-5df8-9681-81abfde85acc.html.

37 Executive Office of the President, Office of Management and Budget, "Statement of Administration Policy, H.R. 2607," October 9, 1997, https://clintonwhitehouse2.archives.gov/OMB/legislative/sap/105-1/HR2607-h.html.

38 Sam Fulwood, "Bill Clears by One Vote, Threatened with Veto," *Los Angeles Times*, October 10, 1997.

39 Robert Greene, "House Narrowly Approves School Vouchers for D.C.," *Chicago Sun-Times*, News pg. 44, October 10, 1997.

40 Ron Hutcheson, "School Vouchers Stir Controversy," Knight-Ridder Newspapers, October 26, 1997.

41 Ibid.

42 Edward J. Boyer, "Blacks Split Over Vouchers," The *Los Angeles Times*, September 3, 2000.

43 Reuters, "GOP Removed Voucher Plan from D.C. Bill," *Rocky Mountain News*, November 14, 1997.

44 Congressional Record, Vol. 143, No. 133, Senate, September 30, 1997.

45 Ibid.

46 Ibid.

47 S.1502 - District of Columbia Student Opportunity Scholarship Act of 1997

48 Carl Rowan, "School-Voucher Plan is a Cruel Sham," *The Buffalo News*, May 2, 1998.

49 Ibid.

50 Terrence Samuel, "Black Ministers Group Comes Out Against School Voucher Proposal," *St. Louis Post Dispatch*, April 1, 1998.

51 Transcript, "Public and Private School Choice in the District of Columbia," Committee on Education and the Workforce, March 12, 1998.

52 Ibid.

53 Ibid.

54 Ibid.

55 Ibid.

56 Ibid.

57 Associated Press, "House Approves Vouchers for D.C. Students," *The State*, May 1, 1998.

58 Rene Sanchez, "District School Voucher Bill Approved," *The Washington Post*, May 1, 1998.

59 Associated Press, "Clinton Kills School Voucher Proposal," *Rocky Mountain News*, May 21, 1998.

60 Paul Pringle, "George W. Bush Addresses Education Reforms," *The Dallas Morning News*, September 3, 1999.

61 Ibid.

62 Associated Press, "Vouchers Split Candidates," *The Trenton Times*, October 3, 2000.

63 Editorial, "Lieberman Solid Pick for Democrats' VP Slot," *San Antonio Express-News*, August 9, 2000.

64 Richard Locker, "Lieberman to 'Debate' Gore But Back Him in Public; School Voucher Stand Put to Rest," *The Commercial Appeal*, August 10, 2000.

65 Ibid.

66 Staff Reports, "School Vouchers, Right or Wrong," *The Times*, February 18, 2001.

67 Andrea Billups, "Supporters Join Bush in Rally for Education Reform Plan," *The Washington Times*, April 13, 2001.

68 Katherine M. Skiba, "Bush Lectures On His School Plan," *Milwaukee Journal Sentinel*, April 13, 2001.

69 Brian DuBose, "Republican Pushes Bill for Vouchers," *The Washington Times*, February 12, 2003.

70 George Archibald, "Paige Calls Bush's Brief in Race Case 'Correct,'" *The Washington Times*, February 5, 2003.

71 Jabeen Bhatti, "Paige's Voucher Bid Gets Rejected; City Rejects Form of School Choice," *The Washington Times*, February 7, 2003.

72 Kelly Amis, "D.C. Parents Call for Vouchers," *School Reform News*, May 1, 2003.

73 Ibid.

74 Erik W. Robelen, "Federal File," *Education Week*, April 9, 2003.

75 Mary Shaffrey, "Williams Endorses Vouchers for Schools," *The Washington Times*, May 2, 2003.

76 "D.C. Mayor Listens to Constituency," *The Winchester Star*, May 10, 2003.

77 Gerald Perseghin, "Witnesses Favor Voucher Funding for D.C. Students," *Catholic Standard*, May 15, 2003.

78 Michelle Malkin, "Eleanor Holmes Norton: The Jailer," Creators Syndicate, May 7, 2003.

79 Deborah Simmons, "It's Not Easy Being Eleanor," *The Washington Times*, May 9, 2003.

80 Humberto Sanchez, "House Panel Oks $7.9B D.C. Bill, Including Voucher Money," The Bond Buyer, July 16, 2003.

81 Bruce Alpert, "Group Explains its Scolding of Landrieu," *The New Orleans Times-Picayune*, September 3, 2003.

82 Alan Fram, "Senate Panel Approves D.C. School Vouchers," Associated Press, September 5, 2003.

83 Philip Gailey, "School Vouchers are Dividing Democrats in Washington, D.C.," *St. Petersburg Times*, September 7, 2003.

84 Congressional Record, Volume 149, No. 134, September 26, 2003.

85 George Archibald, "D.C. Vouchers Face Senate Test," *The Washington Times*, September 11, 2003.

86 Matthew Vadum, "House Passes $7.8B D.C. Spending Bill, Including $10 M for Vouchers," Thomson Media, September 11, 2003.

87 Coalition for Accountable Public Schools, "D.C. Community Members Express Outrage at Newest Voucher Legislation," Coalition for Accountable Public Schools Press Release, June 24, 2003.

88 ACLU, "ACLU Urges Congress to Reject Voucher Scheme in the District of Columbia," ACLU Press Release, June 24, 2003. American Federation of Teachers, "Statement from Sandra Feldman, President of the American Federation of Teachers, On the House Government Reform Committee Hearing On School Voucher Proposal. For the District of Columbia," American Federation of Teachers Press Release, June 24, 2003.

89 Ibid.

90 Ralph Neas, "Dear Representative Letter," People for the American Way, June 24, 2003.

91 Stop D.C. Vouchers, "D.C. Parents Denounce Rep. Tom Davis' New Voucher Bill," Stop D.C. Vouchers Press Release, June 24, 2003.

92 Lolita C. Baldor, "Kennedy Pledges to Defeat School Voucher Bill," Associated Press, September 12, 2003.

93 George Archibald, "D.C. Vouchers Face Senate Test," *The Washington Times*, September 11, 2003.

94 Jo-Ann Moriarty, "D.C. Ad Hits Kennedy Stand," *The Republican*, September 6, 2003.

95 Editorial, "Kennedy Shameful on D.C. Voucher Bill," *Boston Herald*, September 13, 2003.

96 Caroline Hendrie and Erik W. Robelen, "Senate Still Wrangling Over D.C. Voucher Plan," *Education Week*, October 1, 2003, https://www.edweek.org/ew/articles/2003/10/01/05voucher.h23.html.

97 Spencer S. Hsu, "Williams Touts Vouchers," *The Winchester Star*, September 25, 2003.

98 Ibid.

99 Brian DeBose, "GOP Undecided if Vouchers Will be in Omnibus Bill," *The Washington Times*, November 13, 2003.

100 Matthew Vadum, "House Approves Omnibus Spending Bill, But Senate May Put Off Final OK," Thomson Media, December 9, 2003.

101 Spencer Hsu, "Bill Funding D.C. Vouchers for Schools Clears Congress," *The Washington Post*, January 23, 2004.

102 Office of the Press Secretary, "President Pleased Senate Passes Omnibus Budget Bill," The White House, January 22, 2004.

103 Derrill Holly, "Huge Demand for School Vouchers in Capital City," Associated Press, June 11, 2004.

104 Jason Richwine, "D.C. Voucher Students: Higher Graduation Rates and
     Other Positive Outcomes," The Heritage Foundation, July 28, 2010.
     https://www.heritage.org/education/report/D.C.-voucher-students-
     higher-graduation-rates-and-other-positive-outcomes

105 Drew Atchison and Laura Stein, "Looking Back to Move Forward:
     Progress and Opportunity in District of Columbia Public Schools,"
     American Institutes for Research, September 2017.

106 Curtis Brennan, "Radio Ads Ask Whether Kerry Takes Blacks for
     Granted," *Milwaukee Journal Sentinel*, August 15, 2004.

107 Tony Cox, "Interview: Thomas Edsall, Virginia Walden-Ford and
     Congresswoman Stephanie Tubbs-Jones discuss political ad wars," Tavis
     Smiley on NPR, August 16, 2004.

108 Timothy Noah, "The GOP Minstrel Show," *Slate*, August 12, 2004.

109 Clarence Page, "Bush Values Got More Black Votes," *Chicago Tribune*,
     November 7, 2004.

110 Kristen Chick, "Future of D.C. School Vouchers Worries Parents," *The
     Washington Times*, July 29, 2007.

111 Editorial, "A Boost for D.C. Schools," *The Washington Post*, February 3,
     2008.

112 Marion Barry, "Choices for D.C. Parents," *The Washington Post*, May
     13, 2008.

113 Greg Rosalsky, "Obama Administration Softens Position on D.C.
     Voucher Program," *Huffington Post*, June 18, 2012, https://www.
     huffpost.com/entry/obama-D.C.-voucher-program_n_1606981.

114 Newsmax.com, "D.C. School Voucher Program in Jeopardy," *Newsmax*,
     February 28, 2009.

115 Dan Lips and Lindsey Burke, "Politicians Should Value Education of
     Average American Children," *Collegiate Times*, April 28, 2009.

116 Elizabeth Hillgrove, "Senate Kills GOP's D.C. Vouchers Bid," *The
     Washington Times*, March 11, 2009.

117 Gary Emerling, "Vouchers in D.C. to Get Reprieve," *The Washington
     Times*, May 7, 2009.

118 Anthony A. Williams and Kevin P. Chavous, "The Man Who Can Save
     D.C.'s Educational Lifeline," *The Washington Post*, December 4, 2009,
     http://voices.washingtonpost.com/local-opinions/2009/12/the_man_
     who_can_DCs_educationa.html.

119 Heritage Foundation, "Save the D.C. Opportunity Scholarship Program," YouTube, February 24, 2009, https://www.youtube.com/watch?v=QKzZJoPu1OQ.

120 Ibid.

121 James Oliphant, "School Voucher Program May be Allowed to Expire," *Chicago Tribune*, March 11, 2009.

122 Reason TV, "What We Saw at the D.C. Voucher Rally," YouTube, May 12, 2009, https://www.youtube.com/watch?v=V34kYMm82oo.

123 Ibid.

124 Ibid.

125 American Federation for Children, "D.C. School Choice: Students Speak Out in Favor of D.C. Opportunity Scholarship Program," YouTube, May 8, 2009, https://www.youtube.com/watch?v=k5maC3KX6Nc.

126 Ibid.

127 Mary Katharine Ham, "Meet the 'Save Our D.C. Opportunity Scholarship' Activists," *The Washington Examiner*, May 6, 2009.

128 Gary Emerling, "Vouchers in D.C. to Get Reprieve," *The Washington Times*, May 7, 2009.

129 Bill Turque, "Hearing Pours Praise on Voucher Program for D.C. Students in Private Schools," *Washington Post*, May 14, 2009.

130 Laura Wright, "New Poll Shows Support for D.C. Opportunity Scholarship Program," Catholic Standard, July 29, 2009.

131 Kristi Joudan, "Parents Rally for Vouchers," *The Washington Times*, August 21, 2009.

132 D.C. Parents for School Choice, "Dramatic Standoff at U.S. Department of Education as Six D.C. School Voucher Backers Block Doorway," D.C. Parents for School Choice, September 8, 2009.

133 Dan Lips, "Civil Disobedience for Educational Opportunity," National Review, September 8, 2009.

134 Archdiocese of Baltimore, "More than 1,000 Students Rally at Capitol for School Vouchers," September 30, 2009, https://www.archbalt.org/more-than-1000-students-rally-at-us-capitol-for-school-vouchers/?print=print.

135 American Federation for Children, "Save School Choice Rally 9/30/09: Carmen Holassie," YouTube, October 11, 2009, https://www.youtube.com/watch?v=TL0bWQsdOyw.

136 American Federation for Children, "Latasha Bennett Calls on Congress and President Obama to Save D.C. School Choice," YouTube, October 11, 2009, https://www.youtube.com/watch?v=gkGYxuzq9rE.

137 American Federation for Children, "Howard Fuller Calls on President Obama to Save D.C. School Choice," YouTube, October 11, 2009, https://www.youtube.com/watch?v=gnPndrUZg3M.

138 Robert Tomsho, "D.C. School Vouchers Have a Brighter Outlook in Congress," *The Wall Street Journal*, October 19, 2009.

139 Carol E. Lee, "Boehner to Push School Vouchers," *Politico*, January 24, 2011.